W9-BBE-492

ISBN 90 247 1655 1

PRINTED IN THE NETHERLANDS

# FROM SUBSTANCE TO SUBJECT

## Studies in Hegel

*by*

NATHAN ROTENSTREICH

MARTINUS NIJHOFF / THE HAGUE / 1974

"Kant is quoted with admiration, that he taught *philosophizing* not *philosophy*; as if somebody taught carpentry, but not to make a table, chair, door, cupboard etc."

From: Hegels Aphorismen aus Jenenser Zeit, in: Karl Rosenkranz: *Georg Wilhelm Friedrich Hegels Leben*, Darmstadt 1963, p. 552.

For Paul Weiss

"For length of days and years of life
and peace, shall they add to thee".

"Aboth", ("Fathers"), VI, 7.

# TABLE OF CONTENTS

# AUTHOR'S NOTE

The present book is concerned with an analysis of Hegel's own rendering of the thrust of his system: The *fundamental principle,* he says in one of his Aphorisms, of a system of philosophy is its *result.* The book analyses the various renderings of the shift from the category of substance to totality of subject. These shifts are to exemplify the status of the result as the first principle. To be sure, the analytic interpretation of the texts is accompanied by a critical evaluation of the attempt and its alleged success.

The analysis, interpretation and critique presented here are based mainly on Hegel's own texts. To the extent secondary literature is introduced and consulted, the author wishes to express his preference for Hegel's contemporaries and immediate disciples, mainly Johann Eduard Erdmann (1805–1892) and Karl Rosenkranz (1805–1870), and between the two Rosenkranz is given priority. The reason for this preference is not related to the real or alleged fact that the two philosophers were middle-of-the-road Hegelians (and one may doubt whether this applies to Rosenkranz at all) and that the middle-of-the-road position is necessarily sound and level-headed. The reason lies rather in the fact that the two philosophers had a very clear empathy with Hegel's system and attempted to recapitulate Hegel's own reasoning more than overload it with interpretations. They really drank from the same spring. The present-day secondary literature is consulted in so far as it focuses on critical issues like concept and time, though this concentration in turn reflects in some measure issues which are in the forefront of present-day philosophical controversies. This literature is inclined to look at Hegel in retrospect.

The author is indebted to Mrs. Rita Saphir-Braun who in her habitual way helped him in the preparation of the manuscript.

Miss Judith Feinstein gave the manuscript its final shape and thanks are due to her.

Jerusalem, 1972.

# A NOTE ON REFERENCES

Hegel's *Wissenschaft der Logik* is referred to as *Logik* and quoted from Georg Lasson's edition, Leipzig 1923. I – refers to Erster Teil; II – refers to Zweiter Teil. In brackets (I or II) references are given to: *Hegel's Science of Logic*, translated by W. H. Johnston and L. G. Stuthers, with an Introductory Preface by Viscount Haldane of Cloan, London 1961.

*Phänomenologie des Geistes* is quoted from the Georg Lasson's edition, Leipzig 1921, as *Phänomenologie*.

*Encyklopädie der Philosophischen Wissenschaften im Grundrisse*, is referred to as: *Encykl.* and quoted by paragraphs: §. Wherever the reference is to the *Zusätze* it is said: *Zusatz*, with the number of the respective paragraph.

All other quotations from Hegel are from: *Sämtliche Werke* edited by Hermann Glockner. The references are to S. W. and the respective volume (I, II, etc.). Kant's *Kritik der reinen Vernunft* is quoted as *Kr.d.r.V.*, B. In brackets (Kemp Smith) refers to: *Critique of Pure Reason*, translated by Norman Kemp Smith, New York and Toronto, 1965.

# CHAPTER ONE

## CORRELATION AND TOTALITY

### I

Hegel's well-known saying[1] that mediation or detour is the way of the Spirit can be applied pointedly to the issue at hand – that the True is not substance but just as much subject.

As a matter of fact, terminologically speaking, "substance" and "subject" have the same meaning. Both are Latin renderings of the Greek *"hypokeimenon."* Substance, *substantia*, is essence, that which subsists in itself, the status of the thing in its independence. Subject, *subiectus*, is that which underlies, which is underneath, in which qualities inhere, and of which qualities are predicated in propositions. It is this latter meaning of subject which has turned it into a grammatical term. "Underlying" or "lying below" is also expressed when we say "subject to something" or use "subject" to mean a member of a state. Thus both substance and subject denote a foundation, which is open to changes, interpretations and attributions. Leibniz understood *"Selbstand,"* substance, as the self-contained position, so that both substance and subject can be viewed as fulfilling its conditions.

Philosophical tradition has brought about a separation between substance and subject. Substance has retained its original meaning of essence, that which underlies, while subject has come to mean the sum total of perceptions, images and feelings, that is, consciousness. Thus we use "subjective" in its current sense, whereas in the traditional sense subject is not at all subjective – personal, erratic, impressionistic – but substantive.

Mind came to be seen as a subject in which ideas inhere in the way qualities inhere in substance. At this point substance and subject ceased to be synonymous philosophical terms. Substance was placed

[1] *S.W.*, XVII, p. 66.

in the order of things, and subject in the order of Ego or mind, or else Ego in Kant's sense, the unity of subject.[2] In Kant's sense, subject and consciousness are identical; consciousness is conceived of by Kant, as well as by Hegel, as the relation of the Ego to its objects.

Against this background one may present the thesis that Hegel's system is an attempt to reconcile substance and subject, retaining substance as essence and subject as consciousness or cognition. The reconciliation does not blot out the distinctions wrought in the course of philosophical development; it retains these distinctions while applying itself to a synthesis in which object is Ego and Ego is object.

Hegel uses a strong word, corruption (*das Verderben*)[3] when expressing his view that philosophy is a redemption of that which had gotten lost en route, or a reclaiming of what had been corrupted. The attempt to reconcile substance and subject can be said to epitomize his programmatic view of the nature of philosophy.

The purpose of the present analysis is to work out in detail Hegel's attempted reconciliation of substance and subject. This calls for an analysis of the stages in the dialectical explication by which Hegel moves toward his goal. It calls for consideration of the course pursued by Hegel in its systematic aspect as well as in its various historical contexts. Finally, it calls for a critical examination both of Hegel's overall objective and of the details of the procedure whereby he aims at this objective.

If we take into account the religious background of Hegel's thought, something else attracts our notice. At an early stage in Christian thought, subject acquired the meaning of person. In the history of Christian speculation about the Trinity, the notion of Person (*Persona*) arose as a kind of corrective to the notions of substance and the substantive unity of God. The notion of substance lacked personal character and could be viewed merely as essence, being or *ousia*. In attempting a reconciliation between substance and subject, Hegel retained some of the motivation found in Christian tradition, though he gave it a speculative turn peculiar to him. Whether this turn preserves the spirit of the tradition, even though obliterating the letter, will be one of the supplementary issues of our discussion.[4]

---

[2] *Kr.d.r.V.*, A p. 356 (Kemp-Smith p. 338).

[3] *S.W.*, XVII, p. 82.

[4] Helmut Thielicke, "Was meint das Wort 'Gott'? Über Relevanz und Verbindlichkeit des Theos in der Theologie," in *Studium Generale* 23 (1970) p. 134.

2

Hegel tries to join to the philosophical position which places totality within the reach of cognition proper, the idea that totality is within the realm of immanence and thus open to knowledge. This combination tries, in fact, to overcome the dilemma of Kant, for whom metaphysics is merely the pretention of knowing totality. Knowledge of totality cannot be attained, according to Kant, since knowledge is of its nature partial. The only possible knowledge is knowledge of partialities, through functional concepts unified by means of the categories and laws applied to them. Hegel, on his part, tries to show that totality can be encompassed by knowledge. Since he accepts Kant's association of knowledge with immanence, totality is thus placed within the realm of immanence. Immanence does not amount to a sum total of partial subject matters interrelated by the function of Reason as imposer of laws; the immanent may contain totality. The elaboration of this view produces what is central in Hegel's philosophy, namely, the shift from the concept of substance to the concept of subject.

Let us pause at the notion of "totality within the realm of immanence," or, more briefly, "immanent totality." Totality, or else its synonyms like "the whole" (*Allheit, universitas*) is a central notion in Kant's theory of Dialectic. Any expression of a totality of an idea arising out of a "synthesis of the conditions of all possible things in general" is called by Kant an Ideal. An Ideal is a fully determined idea of an "all of reality."[5] For example, the world is the idea of the object of all possible experience, or God is the idea of the being of beings, or the purpose of all purposive things. But totality in general, and Ideal in particular, are beyond the scope of knowledge. They are transcendent, that is to say, are only thought but not known.[6] Transcendent by definition goes or is placed beyond the limits of experience. Therefore such an idea cannot be objectively applied.[7] Hegel's philosophy can be summed up as an attempt to make totality not transcendent, not inapplicable, but immanent and thus within the reach of knowledge. This, of course, calls for a changed understanding of the notion of immanence. Here again, reference to Kant is essential.

For Kant, immanent knowledge is knowledge of nature applicable to

[5] *Kr.d.r.V.*, B pp. 434, 435, 602, 603, (Kemp Smith pp. 385, 489, 490).
[6] *Kr.d.r.V.*, B 497 (Kemp Smith p. 426).
[7] *Kr.d.r.V.*, B p. 671 (Kemp Smith p. 532).

experience (*in concreto*), while transcendent knowledge is concerned with that connection of objects of experience which transcends all experience. Obviously, Hegel does not subscribe to the view that the immanent applies to nature, or to experience in the Kantian sense of unification of perception. For Hegel, whatever is evolving in the whole dialectical procedure is within the reach of knowledge. The immanent is not what is applicable to data but what is within the scope of the explication of concepts. Thus, if totality can be shown to be a dialectical explication of an initial fullness, then totality is immanent and not transcendent. Interestingly enough, Hegel interprets the concept of transcendence so as to fit his own systematic logic. The following is from *Zusatz* to paragraph 42 of the *Encyclopaedia*: "The *transcendent* may be said to be what steps out beyond the categories of understanding; a sense in which the term is first employed in mathematics. Thus in geometry you are told to conceive the circumference of a circle as formed of an infinite number of infinitely small straight lines. In other words, characteristics which the understanding holds to be totally different, the straight line and the curve, are expressly invested with identity. Another transcendent is the self-consciousness which is identical with itself and infinite in itself, as distinguished from the ordinary consciousness which derives its form and tone from finite materials. The unity of self-consciousness, however, Kant called "*transcendental*" only; and he meant thereby that the unity was only in our minds and did not attach to the objects apart from our knowledge of them."

It seems correct to say that here, in a nutshell, Hegel gives to the concept of transcendence a meaning which blurs the distinction between that which is transcendent and that which is immanent. If the transcendent denotes the self-consciousness which is both identical with itself and infinite in itself, then it clearly follows that totality (infinity) lies within self-consciousness. Hegel's allusion to Kant's transcendental unity which is only in our minds, and therefore does *not* contain the infinite-in-itself, corroborates this. Hegel is unquestionably right in his interpretation of Kant. He tries to show that Kant's immanent unity of the consciousness falls short of a full development of that unity. A full development would continue from initial unity to comprehensive unity, from unity as transcendental subject to unity as totality. Hegel's program can be summed up as an attempt so show forth an immanent totality as being not only a projection, but a content proper which can be achieved.

A historical comment will shed some light on the issue before us.

The distinction between immanent and transcendent (*transiens*) as it was made in the Middle Ages can be related to the Aristotelian distinction between acting qua *praxis* and making qua *poiesis*. Action qua *praxis* does not result in an external object or product. It does not "cross over," but remains within the realm of the agent. *Poiesis* produces a separate object, like a ship, for example, and is thus *actio transiens*. What Hegel claims – to be sure, not with regard to the realm of action but with regard to Reason – is that the ultimate object is not outside of Reason, and therefore Reason does not have to get externalized and become *transiens*. If action is understood not as a deed in the practical sense, but as an activity of the Spirit, then the ultimate object is within Reason, and Reason is *actio immanens*. Let us move now to the exploration of the concept of substance (Hegel deals with the concept of substance in the sphere of what is called essence.) In the *Zusatz* to § 111 of the *Encyklopädie* Hegel describes essence as a sphere without a transition. In this sphere, everything is relative. It is composed of relational concepts and different correlations are brought then into relief: essence and appearance, internal and external, force and its expression, law and the content subsumed under it, etc. § 114 states that essence is "essential" only inasmuch as it carries in itself the relation with the other, which, compared to essence, is the non-essential. Essence contains in itself the non-essential element which is also its manifestation – qua *Schein*. Formally speaking, the correlated concepts which compose each distinction qua essential and non-essential, seem to be symmetrical. The two concepts are interdependent; yet the essential element is preferred, while only the non-essential is actually dependent. Thus, essence is both one element of the correlation as well as the whole correlation. Pairing the non-essential element with the essential within the overall sphere of essence raises the non-essential to the level of essence; without the non-essential correlate, essence would cease to be essence. Thus, although the sphere of essence distinguishes between essential and non-essential, at the same time it hints at a totality comprising them both. Distinction and correlation taken separately is not the ultimate stage. Correlation retains, after all, distinction. The ultimate stage is that of totality based on identity. Yet in the sphere of essence we discern the relation of one element to the other: that of force to its manifestations, of law to the data subsumed under it.[8] But the relation to the other is only a transitional stage

---

[8] *Encykl.* § 112.

leading to the relation to oneself (*Selbstbeziehung*). This, the dialectic of the sphere of essence, is only implied by Hegel when he is discussing the category of essence itself within the sphere of essence. It becomes explicit in his analysis of the category of substance within the broad sphere of essence.

3

In a way, Hegel takes over from Kant the notion that the category of substance is one of relation, since substance, in Kant, bears within itself the duality of subsistence and inherence (*substantia et accidens*). Hegel regards this duality as one of the categories of the sphere of essence involved in the dialectic leading from distinction to identity.

At this point it must be asked whether the category of substance is one of those categories where the aspect of relation is more prominent than the aspect of identity, or whether it lies on the threshold of those categories that already exhibit degrees of identity. The question involves a schematic distinction: within the sphere of essence, there are concepts characterized more by relationship than by identity, and there are others which point ahead to the dialectical outcome, in which identity is more prominent than relation.

Substance is the first category in the sphere of actuality within the overall sphere of essence. This position of the category of substance has to be explored, not only for its own sake but also because it can serve as a model for the structure of Hegel's system as a whole.

Among the various aspects of the concept of substance, we distinguish first that of substrate, traditionally tied up with the concept of substance. The substrate is distinguished from the qualities which it carries or which are placed on its surface. Thus the concept of substrate is basic to the distinction between a thing and its properties. Formally, substrate corresponds to essence, while its related qualities correspond to the non-essential correlate within the sphere of essence.

Closer examination of the aspect of substrate reveals that its place "underneath" its accidents is verily outside those qualities which are related to it. It does not depend upon them. It serves as the unifying element *vis-à-vis* their multiplicity. Indeed, this is a paradoxical situation: the substrate is the essential element of the thing and its qualities; yet, it lies underneath in the sense of being outside those qualities, and retains its separate position in their regard. The actual relationship between substrate and qualities does not put an end to this position of separateness. Hence the aspect of substrate in the category of substance does not lead to identity. Kant's emphasis on the aspect of inherence rather than that of subsistence should, let us stress, bring out the idea of relationship, not of identity. Neither can Hegel's category of substance under the aspect of subsistence be viewed as a category which leads to totality based on the intrinsic unity of its elements.

Yet it is the nature of dialectic to overcome the rigid positions taken by concepts. Kant did not apply a dialectical method to his categories, though he did emphasize the third category in each group of categories as a kind of synthesis of the first two. The dialectic as applied by Hegel to the concept of substrate amounts to a virtual removal, or at least radical critique, of that notion. He attempts to sublimate or overcome the aspect of substrate in the category of substance precisely because it brings into relief the inherent contradiction in the concept of substance understood as substrate. This dialectical exposure progresses according to several steps. Let us observe at this point that the overcoming of the aspect of substrate is the precondition for the transition from substance to subject.

4

The first point is this: The rigid distinction between the substrate and the qualities is a contradiction. The substrate, after all, is not located outside or beyond the qualities; it is their ground (*Grund*; in German substrate is *Grundlage* and that term connotes both presupposition and ground).[9] The principal deficiency of the concept of substrate is its abstractness. For Hegel, the very combination of abstractness, which is traditionally viewed as the opposite of concreteness, with essence, is a contradiction. The essence which is abstract turns out to be inessential. The essential element proves to be an inessential circumscription and only an external holding together.[10] Let us trace the development of that contradiction.

The substrate is posited to support a clear-cut distinction between the inner core of things and their external manifestation. The inner core itself is either totally present in the appearing qualities, and thus cannot claim to hold a preferential position *vis-à-vis* those qualities, or else it is abstract and empty and thus cannot be their underlying

[9] *Logik*, p. 110 (II, p. 116).
[10] *Ibid.*, p. 113 (II, p. 119).

essence. What actually happens is that the essential element shifts from the correlate of essence to the qualities themselves. Thingness (*Dingheit*) passes over into quality.[11] Substrate loses its independence along with its essential position. The shift leads to that facet of "thing-ness" which Hegel characterizes as "too" or "also" (*auch*),[12] just the sum total of qualities. In so far as the substrate, which was originally posited as the underlying essence of things, turns out to be the sum total of the qualities of things, it has shown itself to be an abstraction, and is subject to the criticism of abstraction which runs through Hegel's entire system. Mere abstraction is true to the same extent as mere nothing is true.[13]

The non-dialectical feature in the rigid notion of substrate is found precisely in its separation from its qualities. Substrate is called pejo-ratively, "the quiet thing of many features." It lacks dynamic quality, since a dynamic factor requires relation between definite elements, and substrate lacks any definiteness of its own. To be consistent, dialectical reasoning must show that an aloof position can be attributed to sub-strate only from the angle of external observation, but not from that of real reasoning.

The problem faced here is as follows: Substrate amounts to the negation of its own qualities. But, how can a negative element be a *Grundlage* of positive qualities? Moreover, the substrate as negation presupposes the qualities it negates. Thus it ceases, from this point of view, too, to occupy its alleged preferential position, since in order to know what the substrate as negation is, we must first presuppose the negated qualities.

Once it became clear that the concept of substrate could not perform its supposed function, Hegel set about an attempt of a different nature, in order to find an inner relationship between pairs of correlated con-cepts. The concept we are to examine next is the concept of law or laws.

The novelty in Hegel's unfolding of his argument lies in the fact that the next step centers on the category of law. True to the duality of essence and its manifestation, the category of law presents a duality of law and phenomena. The law is the essential content of the phe-nomenon. Law has two aspects, the aspect of being a law (*Gesetzsein*) or of being external in terms of the phenomena sub-ordinate to it or the aspect of being identical with itself. In its first aspect, the law ap-

---

[11] *Ibid.*
[12] *Ibid.*, p. 119 (II, p. 125).
[13] *Logik*, I, p. 87. (I, p. 113).

pears in immediate reality and, in so doing, is subjected to accidentality, inessentiality, transition, coming to exist and ceasing to exist. In its aspect as self-identical, the law is the simple content determination, free from change, a permanent element.[14]

5

In the duality of law and phenomena are found the same aspects of permanence and change which were observed with regard to the distinction between substrate and qualities. Substance, the permanent element following the traditional and the Kantian view, is now transformed into law – the concept of law itself is but one of the transformations which the concept of substance in its broad meaning undergoes.

Hegel regards the concept of law as a category, while Kant considered laws as particular expressions of particular categories. Kant draws a distinction between the particular laws of nature, which presuppose perception, and lawfulness in general as the factor necessary for the unification of phenomena in experience,[15] the latter being identical with the sum total of the categories, and the former is not lodged on the level of category at all.

Moreover, Kant distinguishes between changing and permanent, and substance and accident, in terms of time. By introducing the distinction between the level of immediacy, which is governed by processes in time, and the level of essentiality, that of law, which is unrelated to time, Hegel presents law as such as independent of time, or at least initially so. The essence is not in time; only its accidental expressions are.

Hegel's critical analysis of the duality of law and phenomena corresponds to the analysis of substrate and its qualities, only it carries the dialectical discourse a step further. The main critical argument against the aspect of substrate concerned its abstract and empty character. This argument is not valid with regard to the category of law. In the face of what occurs in time, law is determined and distinct in itself.[16] It entails determinateness essentially.[17] We suggest the following interpretation of Hegel's view on this point: each law has its

[14] *Logik*, II, p. 125 (II, pl 131).
[15] *Prolegomena* § 36.
[16] *Logik*, II, p. 125 (II, pp. 130–131).
[17] *Ibid.*

own specific meaning – the law of gravitation, for instance, has its own content which differs as such from the law of entropy or from the laws of evolution. The laws function as regulators of phenomena, but in order to do so they are bound to have some inherent content or characteristic of their own. To some extent, Hegel combines the Platonic view of essences as predicates of things and phenomena with the Kantian view of laws as establishing functional relations between phenomena. Yet this implicit or explicit combination hinders us from restating with regard to law the main argument against the concept of substrate. Since laws do have contents their deficiency cannot lie in their emptiness.

*Pari passu*, we have moved from empty abstraction to determinateness by contents. However, duality is not abolished on the level of law either, since the distinction between the permanent element and the transitory phenomena is retained. The duality which remains is the main categorial argument against the claim that knowledge of law, and of phenomena as governed by law, is the ultimate stage of cognition. Against the background of this his fundamental argument, Hegel puts forward several specific arguments with regard to the meaning of the content as found in the concept of law. The main point now is the remaining duality in terms of content to be found in the distinction between law and phenomena. Let us list several of these arguments.

The distinction between phenomena governed by laws and these laws themselves is not co-terminous with the distinction between permanence and transition. Phenomena do have their own content which cannot be reduced to the content of the law proper. The law of gravitation, for instance, governs the falling of a stone, but does not cover all the qualities of the stone. The mineralogical nature of the stone, or its geometric shape, is not part of the content of the law, the law being confined to its specific and selective meaning. The partial character of the relation between law and phenomenon brings about a certain externality of law *vis-à-vis* the phenomenon. Phenomena are richer in content than the laws that govern them. Nevertheless, the abstraction inherent in law differs from the abstractness of substrate in that the former is due to a definite, therefore limited, specificity, whereas the latter calls for a total specificity or full determination.

Paradoxically, the law, which corresponds to the essential, is poorer than the phenomenon, which corresponds to the inessential. In addition, the very quality of permanence carries with itself its deficiency: phenomena, which emerge and pass away, are dynamic while the law is static. The quiet (*ruhig*) character of the substrate re-emerges in the law. Law is the quiet copy (*Abbild*). It seems that Hegel's critique of law implies more than would appear from his emphasis on the lack of dynamic quality found in the concept of law. Hegel wanted to stress that law is a copy of the world inasmuch as it presupposes the phenomena it is supposed to govern. Law refers to phenomena but these, in their turn, are independent of the law. What Kant said about laws presupposing perception seems to be reformulated here as an argument against the systematic position of law in the system of knowledge, or in the philosophical system in general.

Another argument deals with the unifying function of law. Law unifies different qualities but cannot prove the necessary character of that unification. Law establishes the necessary relations but it cannot establish its own necessity or the necessity of the relata. Yet we can say from another point of view, that the unified qualities call, necessarily, for this unification. This argument amounts to a positive argument for supplementing the functional validity of law in order to justify affinity between phenomena. This would, at the same time, secure the affinity between the phenomena and the law.

The notion of affinity brings us back to Hegel's point of departure in his progressive interpretation of the diverse aspects of substance. Substance as substrate and substance as the permanent relations between the data and phenomena is considered in Hegel's system from the ultimate position of identity. The question arises whether identity has been achieved on the level of these concepts or not. Critical exploration has revealed, clearly, that identity has not been achieved. Neither the category of substrate nor that of law can provide a correlation which could reach beyond its elements to a full and self-contained identity. Kant, unlike Hegel, is concerned mainly with the transcendental deduction or mediating schematism. He does not question the validity of the law. Kant's concern presupposes a duality between a valid law and the phenomena to which the valid law is applied. Insofar as such a duality is presupposed – this is Hegel's reasoning – philosophy is not dealing with knowledge of the Absolute, but with knowledge of subjectivity, or, with critique of the faculty of knowledge.[18]

The structure we have just uncovered, together with its inherent shortcomings, pertains also to notion of force and its manifestations.

[18] *S. W.*, I, p. 296.

The sphere of force is entirely bound up in reciprocal assumptions, that is to say, force assumes its expressions while the expressions assume their force. Hegel drives this idea home in several ways. He says that force is a conditioning factor, a mutual impetus (*Anstoss*) against the other force with regard to which it is active. Forces mutually challenge each other, influence and instigate each other (*sollizitierend* and *sollizitiert*).[19] Hegel's description of forces in action reveals that absence of identity is also characteristic of the realm of force. The most that can be attributed to that realm is mutuality of attraction and repulsion, but by no means identity between the factors embraced.

It is not on the level of functional relations between data but on the level of comprehensive totality that the true and real meaning of the category of substance should and can be looked for. Substance should be regarded as an essential element placed in such a mode of correlation with the quasi non-essential, that totality would be explicated out of this merger.

The categories of substrate and law are the two aspects which were traditionally found in the category of substance. Hegel points to the limited and limiting meaning of these two categories and establishes the category of substance proper, a category which will be free from the systematic deficiencies adhering to both substrate and permanence qua law or else force and its manifestations. The category of substance is endowed with a systematic priority compared with the two concepts we explored immediately after it, though the identity we are seeking is still not fully established. Hence a further move is necessary and that amounts to the shift from substance to subject.

6

In other words: As long as the terms are only correlated, as is the case with substrate and qualities, or with law and the phenomena governed by it, their relationship is accidental, lacking necessity. Traditionally – here again Hegel draws from tradition – substance is the necessary being, presupposed for the sake of qualities. Yet necessity implies not only a position but also the inner connection between the qualities pertaining to substance. Indeed, the concept of absolute necessity is the closest point of reference for the category of substance. Absolute necessity implies identity between the relata. The acciden-

---

[19] *Logik*, II, p. 147 (II, p. 151).

tality is the absolute necessity, or, stated differently, the identity of the
being in its negation with itself is substance.[20] Substance is relation to
itself rather than relation to the other, be that other the qualities to
which the substrate is related or the phenomena to which the law is
related. Self-relation supersedes correlation, and the sphere thus delineated is that of totality. Totality replaces duality, identity replaces
mutual interdependence of relata – and indeed this is the point Hegel
is trying to make.

How do we assess the identity reached at this stage? Hegel is concerned to show that necessity is not emptiness. On the contrary, it is
Being full of content (*inhaltsvolles Wesen*),[21] a wealth of content.[22]
Identity between the relata could not be established previously in the
dialectical development, either because the substrate is lacking content
or because the law is endowed with limited and rigid content only.
Identifying substance with the whole content removes the difficulties
which accompany the correlative concepts. Necessary being must entail
all the content. If not, it would be dependent upon a being or beings
outside itself, and would thus cease to be necessary. It would be an
accidental being to the extent that it was dependent. Thus, necessity
and plenitude of content are two sides of the same coin. In other words,
necessity is inherent in the transition from the internal element to the
external one. Necessity can apply only when there is full identity.
The outcome of this reasoning is that there can be only one substance
in the sense of fullness of content and necessity. At this point, Hegel
was clearly aware that he had moved from Aristotle's concept of substance to that of Spinoza.[23]

The category of substance is superior to the other categories because
it turns qualities and accidents into parts. Substance understood as
totality comprises all those elements which were previously distinct
and separate from the essential element. The concept of a thing
precludes identity since a thing either carries qualities or is subject to a
law. To remedy this Hegel introduces the comparison with light. As
light is not something, not a thing, but its being is its shining, so
manifestation is absolute actuality identical with itself.[24] The use of the
metaphor of light in this context probably has its source in the con-

[20] *Logik*, II, p. 184 (II, p. 187).
[21] *Encykl.* § 149.
[22] *Ibid.*, § 151.
[23] *Logik*, I, p. 100 (I, p. 126); Consult: *Encykl.* § 151.
[24] *Logik*, II, p. 185 (II, p. 187).

ception which Hegel shared with his time, that light is a force filling space and as such is neither a thing nor a substrate.

The metaphor of light, however, bears the traditional associations connected with the identification of light with the good and God. Hegel hesitated to identify substance with light, in the sense that light was taken in the "Metaphysics of Light" of Plato and the mystics. He did use this metaphor, but after all, substance is not the ultimate and highest stage in the evolvement of his system.

In rejecting correlations, characteristic of the preceding stages of knowledge, and in using the metaphor of shining, Hegel asserts that substance is the identity of *Erscheinungen*, and includes accidentality in itself. The accidentality is the substance itself. While the category of law exhibited the pattern of subjection, the category of substance exhibits the pattern of comprehension – comprehension understood in two senses: as entailment and as cognition, as the German *"begreifen"* would suggest. Hegel goes beyond the position of substance as category of relation, since identity is posited not simply as relation but as self-relation, or, in Hegel's own terminology, as absolute relation. It must be observed that Hegel does not mean by substance the totality of attributes only, or the essential traits of substance in the sense Spinoza used the notion of attribute. He refers to accidents in the traditional sense as the transitory and fortuitous, the original meaning of accident being that which comes into being suddenly or unexpectedly.

7

Does this characterization of the category of substance make for the conclusion that in substance the ultimate systematic concept is presented? Is the full totality established, and the notion of totality exhausted to the ultimate? The category of substance is lodged within the sphere of essence, which means that it still bears traces of dualities that have not yet been fully overcome; or, it bears traces of the traditional distinctions, made in terms of content and status, between substance and its accidents. This is the case in spite of the fact that within the category of substance there is a continuous flow from substance to accidents.

The concept of substance still has a correlate-accidents. Hegel speaks of a to-be-separable-aspect of substance, referring to substance as being identical with itself, being in-itself and for-itself, and thus separate from the totality of accidents. The verbal distinction between sub-

stance and accident is perpetuated despite the development of substance as true totality of accidents. The nominal traces are seen at
least as a formal distinction between the relata. Thus the concept of
substance still evokes dualistic associations despite Hegel's attempt
to establish an identity which would comprehend both terms. The
problem of the category of substance is tied up with the transition
from absolute necessity to substance. Necessity is the actuality the
necessary being as *causa sui*. Here, too, Hegel follows Spinoza. The
relation between substance and accidents consists in a constant flow
from the former to the latter. But the position of substance as independent and necessary is what counts. The meaning of substance must
be considered not only from the angle of the relationship between it
and its accidents, but also in terms of the modal status which inheres
in the substance proper and not in the sum total of accidents.

This latent preference of substance over its accidents comes to the
fore in that aspect of substance which Hegel calls "the aspect of force,"
which we have already mentioned. Substance is manifested as creative
in the turning of the possible into the actual, or, from the opposite end,
as destructive insofar as it turns actuality into possibility. In both
directions substance exhibits its power over accident, while the accidents as such have no power over each other.[25] Both as constructive
and as destructive, substance has a role which cannot be attributed to
accident. Thus the full identity between substance and accidents is not
realized since the nominal and formal traces of previous distinctions are
still retained. Substance being the point of departure as cause of itself
and as embodiment of power – there is only one-way passage from it to
accident. From accident to substance there is no passage, at least under
the aspects of *causa sui* and power. Hegel is implying that the idea of
source and origin is still inherent in the category of substance, in fact,
essence turns out to be source and origin. To that extent substance still
remains within the sphere of essence, though it points, more than do
the preceding categories, beyond the stage of essence with its duality
or correlation, to the stage of actuality as identity. Perhaps Hegel
himself oscillates between taking the category of substance as presenting identity – this view would be expressed in the metaphor of light –
and taking it as embodying the independent and self-contained. The
course of the dialectic as a whole gives reason to suppose that the
second view is to be preferred. The notion of substrate undergoes many

25 *Logik*, II, p. 187 (II, p. 189).

transformations *en route*, but it is retained, even on the level of the category of substance, as a dynamic *Grund* or force. All and all we see time and again that Hegel clinging to the notion of substance points to its shortcomings: totality proper is not arrived at and Hegel's different modes of arguing aim at this negative conclusion. The totality is bound to be a dynamic one, and the explanation for its dynamic character is found in the aspect of force. Yet, Hegel is still looking for a further category which will yield a totality dynamic in itself, and which will thus go beyond such dynamics as are accounted for by the dependence of the sum-total of accidents on substance.[26]

Summing up this part we may say: The concept of absolute necessity served as the logical ground for the category of substance. But substance cannot be viewed as identical with the Absolute, since the Absolute has to be viewed as overcoming all duality. Within the sphere of dualities and correlations, the Absolute would be merely one of the correlates and not the actual fullness. This seems to be the principal reason for the various stages in Hegel's dialectical presentation of the concept of substance.

[26] The preponderance of the essential element in the sum total of the correlation is stated by Karl Rosenkranz as follows: the categories of essence are concepts of reflection, that is to say, they can be thought as such without their opposites. See: Karl Rosenkranz, *Metaphysik, Wissenschaft der Logik*, 1. Teil, Königsberg, 1858, p. 279. Again, in emphasizing the primacy of substance Karl Rosenkranz observes that in German the term substance connotes the thing, *die Sache*. In the word *Ursache* (cause) that metaphysical character is even more prominent. *Ibid.*, p. 453.
Consult: Andrew J. Reck: Substance, Subject and Dialectic, incl. in: *Tulane Studies in Philosophy vol. ix, Studies in Hegel*, Tulane University, New Orleans, 1960, pp. 109 ff. On the transition from Kant to Hegel related to the notion of Idea see the present author's: Ideas and Ideal, incl. in: *The Legacy of Hegel, Proceedings of the Marquette Symposium 1970*, edited by J. J. O'Malley e.a. Martinus Nijhoff, The Hague, 1973 pp. 288 ff.

# CHAPTER TWO

# THE BEGINNING AND THE RESULT

## I

The criticism of the category of substance in terms of its position in the system runs in two interconnected directions. The first leads to a further category which will be free from the preference given to the relatum of substance as opposed to that of accident. It leads to interdependence. The second direction is not categorial in the limited sense of that term; it links the system with the concept of subject. Let us deal with these two directions of Hegel's argument.

The logical precondition for totality to amount to identity, and not merely correlation, is complete symmetry between the relata or parts comprising the totality. To give to the sum total of accidents the same position given to substance requires that the category of mutuality replace the category of substance. The category of mutuality grants equal activity to both relata, removing the preponderance given to one. Mutuality is a reciprocal causality of substances and their accidents conditioning each other. Each relatum is at once active and passive with regard to the other. Since both are thus, any difference between them is removed.[1] Full totality is full reciprocity between the elements of which the totality consists. Thus the category of substance is only a stage on the way to totality. Totality entails repleteness of substance with its accidents. It elevates that repleteness to the position of a complete circle whose elements are mutually, and not one-sidedly, dependent.

A comparison with Kant's table of categories is appropriate at this point. Under categories of relation, Kant has substance, causality and dependence, and finally community as reciprocity between the active

---

[1] *Logik*, II, p. 202 (II, p. 204).

and the passive.[2] Yet when he formulates the third Analogy he speaks of all substances insofar as they can be perceived to coexist in space as standing in permanent relation of mutuality or reciprocity toward one another.[3] Kant does not look at mutual action as characterizing a comprehensive totality where all parts are mutually dependent. For him, mutuality holds between substances. It is not the nature of the one substance, nor does it bring about a totality. With regard to Kant we may speak about relations between particular things, while with regard to Hegel we may speak about the structure of the universe. Thus we see Hegel move from the category of mutuality to the dialectical exhibition of the concept or of the Idea.

Well-known passages in the Preface to the *Phenomenology of Spirit* refer to both substance and subject, and to the character of the Absolute as determined by them. These statements deserve a historical as well as a systematic analysis.

2

The first text reads as follows:

According to my view, which must justify itself by the presentation of the system, everything depends on this, that we comprehend and express the true not as substance but just as much as subject.[4]

The first point to be noticed is the way Hegel states his program: he does not deny that substance is related to the true, but he suggests that the true be comprehended also as subject. The aspect of substance is retained, but it will be sublated to the aspect of subject.

The second point to be made concerns Hegel's reference to the true and the truth. When he speaks of the true, he is referring to reality or to the Absolute. Why does he employ the terminology of truth? We can assume that this is connected with Hegel's understanding of the concept of truth, which is related to his turning reality, substance, etc., into the concept of subject.

Hegel distinguishes between *Richtigkeit*, which might be rendered into English as correctness, and truth proper. Correctness denotes the

---

[2] *Kr. d. r. V.*, B p. 106 (Kemp-Smith p. 113).

[3] *Ibid.*, B p. 256 (Kemp-Smith p. 233).

[4] The English rendering is from Walter Kaufmann's translation of the Preface to the Phenomenology of Spirit, incl.: Walter Kaufmann, *Hegel* Reinterpretation, Texts and Commentary, Garden City, N. Y. 1965, p. 388. *Phänomenologie des Geistes*, ed. Lasson, Leipzig 1921, p. 12.

formal identity or correspondence of our representation (*Vorstellung*) with its content, whatever that content may be. Truth consists in the correspondence or identity of the object with itself, i.e., with its concept.[5] "Objective thoughts" – this is said in another context – indicate the truth, which is the absolute subject matter of philosophy and not only its goal.[6] Truth, then, inheres in subject matter and not in reflective – external – thinking about subject matter. It is not an attribute of the relation between an external reflection and the object reflected upon, but an attribute of the inner structure of the subject matter itself. Subject matter as identical with its own Idea is truth. Hence: Idea is, first, only universal substance; its true actuality is its development as subject. In this sense we speak about a true man, a true work of art, a true state etc. Subject thus developed is Spirit.

In so far as there is an identity between the concept of actuality and actuality itself, there is awareness or consciousness of that identity. This awareness is present on the level of correctness, where there is correspondence between the representation and the state of affairs represented. It is also present – a fortiori – on the level of truth proper, where the reality as such is aware of its adequacy with its concept. Awareness and concept pertain to subject. On the level of truth proper, since awareness and concept are not outside of the actuality which is conceived, the actuality itself is the subject, knowing itself and knowing that it knows itself. On the level of correctness, the intentionality is conformity of a representation with a given state of affairs. Hence it has a "subjective" connotation. On the level of truth, the intentionality proceeds from actuality to its concept, the conception emerging from the actuality and not from without. It *is* actuality becoming subject. Here, the object becomes the subject, unlike the level of correctness where the subject knows an object outside of itself.

This part of the analysis may be summed up in the dictum: Truth is *adequatio rei et intellectus*. The fully developed concept of *adequatio* is identity. Hence truth is the identity of *res* and *intellectus*. The intellect assesses this identity, since the opaque *res* can be neither identical with the intellect nor conscious of identity. The *adequatio* is therefore moved to the level of intellect. But intellect does not cease to be *res*; it is both *res* and *intellectus* whereby *intellectus* knows its identity with the *res*. *Res* does not disappear; it is the aspect of substance in the totality of

---

[5] *Encykl.* § 172 Zusatz.
[6] *Idem* § 25.

the true; the aspect of *intellectus* is emphasized since the true is better expressed as subject than as substance.

The advantage of the concept of subject over the category of substance lies in what might be called in contemporary philosophical parlance, the phenomenology of subject: subject is intrinsically related to content and there are no contents that do not have a subject. This relation, obtaining by definition between content and subject, removes the residue of duality and mere correlation which cling to the category of substance.

3

The historical context of these considerations is to be found in the systems of Spinoza and Kant. In Hegel's view, Spinozism is the essential origin of all philosophizing[7] – the origin but not the final result of all philosophizing, because in Spinoza substance is only rigid substance, not yet Spirit. Its parts are only modifications of it, not inherently contained in it and cognitively grasped by it.[8] Spinoza's substance lacks the element of negation,[9] which means for Hegel that it lacks identity or manifested with the aspect of non-identity.[10] The reference to identity and non-identity alike is essential, since the two can be comprised by cognition only as interrelated. Hegel re-states the argument of Spinoza's contemporaries that substance cannot lead from unity to multiplicity, but his main argument is that Spinoza's concept of substance does not lead to free subjectivity, or else that subjectivity would have to be outside substance.[11] For Hegel, the evolvement of substance into subject is its transition to the realm of freedom qua Spirit. The shift from substance to subject places totality at the end of the dialectical development and not at its beginning. It amounts to a shift from connected contents to contents comprised in one subject. Hegel attempts to retain the totality inherent in Spinoza's concept of substance by making it a real totality in which both the finitude and the modes of infinity are contents comprised by the one infinite.

*Vis-à-vis* Spinoza, Hegel points to the sublation of substance into subject. *Vis-à-vis* Kant, Hegel points to the realization of subject as substance. Hegel takes issue with Kant with regard to the Paralogisms

[7] *S. W.*, Vol. IXX, p. 376.
[8] *Ibid.*
[9] *Ibid.*, p. 407.
[10] *Logik*, II, p. 42. (II, p. 60).
[11] *Encykl.* § 415.

of Pure Reason.[12] A Paralogism is an invalid syllogism which concludes that the soul is a substance from the premise "I think." Kant argues as follows: the unity of Transcendental Apperception, the unity of the "I think" as vehicle of all concepts, is a logical and therefore formal unity. This is the unity of the subject of my thinking, but not the unity of a subject in the network of experience, because to be involved in the network of experience is to become an object of experience. The Paralogism which turns the subject of thinking into a substance results from the mistaken reasoning that that which cannot be *thought of* but as subject, *exists* as subject, and is thus a substance. What is allowed, is that "I" who think use, myself as subject of the proposition "I think." But this does not say anything about the mode of my existence. What we encounter here is a blurring of the distinction: the abstraction from my empirical existence does not amount to the reality of the thinking self. Kant's principal argument requires that a distinction be maintained between the concept of subject, which has a logical meaning only, and the concept of substance which has a transcendental meaning and is one of the forms unifying the data of experience. The "I" of thinking is not an empirical datum. Thus the category of substance cannot be applied to it. The real is phenomenal, and the logical is not real. Substance relates to the phenomenal; subject relates to the real.

Hegel strongly criticizes Kant's position. Kant, he says, argues against the barbarity of the notions which he repudiates by manifesting the barbarity of his own notions. Kant is right when he says that the "I" is not a soul-thing (*Seelending*), a dead permanent, which has a sensible existence. But he does not present the genuine opposing view, i.e. that the "I" as the universal being of self-thinking is the true reality. Kant regards the category of substance as too high a category to be applied to subject. But the opposite is true. The least that can be said about the "I" or Spirit is that it is "being." In order to apply the concept of being to the concept of subject we must examine both concepts.[13]

Clearly, when substance denotes permanence in time it can be applied to phenomena of experience only but not to the subject of thinking. But when substance denotes totality, and subject denotes the totality of thinking and thoughts and not only the logical unity of thinking, there is a *tertium comparationis* for the identification of substance with

[12] *Kr. d. r. V.*, B pp. 399ff (Kemp-Smith pp. 328ff).
[13] *S. W.*, Vol. IXX, pp. 557ff.

subject, or rather, for the sublation of the category of substance to the level of subject. Substance as presented by Spinoza lacks that self-reflection which belongs to subject. Kant presents the logical subject as a unity but not a totality, because substance cannot be applied to totalities – totality is a metaphysical concept beyond experience – but only to phenomena in time and space. Hegel attempts to bring about a kind of synthesis between Spinoza's "full" substance and Kant's "empty" subject.[14]

### 4

Instead of the term synthesis, we could also use Hegel's favorite term "mediation," mediation being evolving, moving self-identity. There is the evolving identity of the concept and the status of substance with the concept and the status of subject. This identity is not given from the outset; substance in itself is primarily a substrate or the permanent element, while subject is primarily (in the present context, not in the context of the history of the concept where it is identical with substance) the sum-total of the functions and forms of knowledge. The identity between the two is to develop. Hence the Absolute as the actual totality endowed with thinking is the result, not the beginning.

Hegel expresses his conception as follows:

> The whole is only the essence perfecting itself through its development. Of the absolute it should be said that it is essentially result, that it is only in the end what it is in truth; and precisely in this consists its nature: to be actual, subject, or that which becomes itself.[15]

The Absolute means the identity of identity and non-identity, of opposition and being[16] (and Hegel clings to that definition from the very beginning of his philosophical career). Identity of identity and non-identity presupposes their previous development on the level of substrate, law, permanent element, *versus* quality, phenomena and accident. Only when these "first-level" aspects have been developed can they be comprehended in the totality of identity and non-identity. They represent tentative attempts to achieve totality which must

[14] Consult the present author's: *Experience and its Systematization*, Studies in Kant, The Hague 1965, pp. 44ff (The second enlarged edition of that book, The Hague, 1972 contains an analysis of the concept of substance in Kant and its transformation in Hegel, pp. 132ff).
[15] *Phänomenologie*, p. 14, translation p. 390.
[16] *S. W.*, I, p. 124.

precede the achievement of totality on the level of subject. Not only is the ultimate evolvement of the Absolute significant, but the process as well. We shall deal presently – first – with the significance of process with regard to the turn from substance into subject, and – second – with regard to Hegel's concept of Spirit and his view of the nature of philosophy.

The "Absolute" originally denotes that which does not depend upon anything outside of itself. The aspect independence brought about the identification of the Absolute with the perfect, and led further, as with Nicolaus Cusanus, to the application of the term Absolute to God. It goes without saying that Hegel changed the initial meaning of the term Absolute. Once the Absolute is viewed as a result, it is no longer independent but comprehends in itself all aspects of the structure of the concept. The Absolute is viewed as a totality and not as a separate entity. Here again Hegel tries to show that the Absolute, which Kant took to be transcendent, is not transcendent since it includes in itself all the stages of the evolvement of the concept. The Absolute is true since truth means the correspondence of concept to reality – the Absolute alone corresponds to the concept of reality by being full reality. The sense of truth which Hegel uses here, of course, is again not that of correctness, but of the inner adequacy of reality. It is this inner adequacy of reality which leads to identity between reality and thinking. Thus, the statement that the true is the whole amounts to the statement that the true is subject, or that reality is subject.

Once "truth" is presented in this way, we cannot assume that we do not know the truth. The meaning of truth is that I know what something is. The more I know, the more the features of reality come to light. The more the features of reality come to light, the more I know. Truth is progressively realized, realized in the objective sense of becoming actual and in the subjective sense of becoming known. We know the truth when we know the Spirit in its process of self-realization.

Hegel's view of philosophy follows this vein. Philosophy is concerned with the knowledge of the Spirit and its self-realization, and philosophy is itself part and parcel of that same realization. The true is a system comprising both the actuality of the world and the conceptual self-understanding of the world, i.e., the self-understanding which is accomplished in the philosophical system.

Marx characterizes, in a critical vein to be sure, the "Leitmotiv" of Hegel's system as a view of the real as the result of thinking, thinking which becomes more and more comprehensive, deeper and deeper,

moving always out of its own momentum.[17] We would suggest some
amendment to Marx's characterization: contents become deeper and
deeper by becoming more and more known. The deepened contents
become, in turn, transitional stages in the further development of
contents, through awareness of these contents. There is both development and accumulation in Hegel's system. In other words: substance
is not rejected. It is sublated.

Underlying this accumulative dynamic is the idea that there are no
ready-made contents present in advance of consciousness. Hegel begins with a synthesis between contents and thinking of contents. The
ultimate category of subject can be recognized as ultimate because the
initial stage is a synthesis which already points toward it. As we move
from synthesis to further synthesis, the end is more concretely exhibited. This, as a matter of fact, is the shape of dialectic in Hegel, as
we shall see in a later stage of our exploration. We may note here that
in starting with the dynamic affinity between contents and thinking,
Hegel rejects Kant's theory of synthesis as well as Fichte's "I" and
Schelling's philosophy of the dynamics of nature, in so far as this
conception of nature plays a significant role in Schelling's philosophy
of nature. The Absolute as a result is by the same token an end, a *telos*
of the whole evolvement. To some extent every stage which precedes
the achievement of the Absolute can be viewed as a means to the end,
yet every stage, since it is preserved in the subsequent stage, is not
only a means to but a part of the ultimate totality. The stages are, on
the one hand, methodical classifications on our part, and on the other
hand, substantive components. The dynamic of the end is present in
the dynamic of the process; the activity of the end pervades the process.
Real actuality conforming to its idea is perennially present; any truth
known is known as true because of the presence of the idea. The process
leading to the end does not create the end. It only makes explicit its
contents.

5

In this light, it is necessary to qualify Hegel's programmatic statement
about the Absolute as result. Explication is the deed of the Absolute
itself. It starts with itself and reaches its consummation with itself.[18]

---

[17] "Einleitung zur Kritik der Politischen Ökonomie," Karl Marx – Friedrich Engels,
*Werke vol. 13*, Berlin, 1961, p. 632.
[18] *Logik*, II, p. 160 (II, p. 164).

The Absolute can be a result because it is present from the beginning in an initial shape, content and self-awareness. *En route* it only becomes more developed and more comprehended. In other words, we move from a latent synthesis to an articulate one.

Spontaneity is required here. For Kant, spontaneity had the specific meaning of the mind's power of producing representations from itself.[19] He limited spontaneity to the unification of the manifold of representations. Hegel does not view Reason as the faculty which unifies the manifold. Reason, and Spirit at that, is the development of the manifold out of its own resources. As he says, things are what they are through the activity of the concept which is inherent in them and which reveals itself in them.[20] The activity of the concept in Hegel is Kant's spontaneity written large. Whereas in Kant, spontaneity refers concepts to data, in Hegel spontaneity, as the activity of concept, forms the very data out of its own activity.

Spontaneity can be viewed as the medium in which the whole system takes shape. It is the presupposition and the momentum leading from one step to another. Yet a fundamental question may be raised: wherein lies the guarantee that spontaneity will lead to the end *qua* subject? After all, spontaneity might give rise to scattered concepts with no inner principle giving them the form of a system. Hegel had to wrestle with that possibility and to add an element to spontaneity which would give it a certain character. He infuses the element of awareness of the proposition (*der Satz*) in the form of a judgement since judgement per se lacks the capacity of expressing speculative truths. The judgement is an identical relation between a subject and a predicate. Yet in this case it is abstracted from the fact that the subject may have, in addition, more determinations than those entailed in the predicate; it is abstracted also from the fact that the predicate is wider than the subject. The lack of identity between the subject and the predicate is not expressed in the judgement; only their identity is expressed.[21] The first comment to be made here – to realize Hegel's intention – is that there is no judgement without an accompanying reflection on the judgement. From the variety of possible determinations which could be attributed to a subject we select, as it were, the determination expressed in the particular predicate before us. We contract the meaning of the subject to the predicate attached to it

[19] *Kr. d. r. V.*, B p. 75 (Kemp-Smith p. 93).
[20] *Encykl.* § 163.
[21] *Logik*, I, p. 76 (I, p. 103).

specifically. We are aware of the breadth both of the subject and its predicates, and we establish the connection between them against the background of their respective breadths. In formulating the judgement we know that we perform a limitation. This knowledge is an expression of spontaneity, since we overcome and move beyond the limitation by the very act of knowing it, but fot that matter, the very limitation is also a product of spontaneity.

Reflection on the limitation of breadth which occurs in the formulation of propositions and judgements has a guiding role in the subsequent stage of formulation of the concept. Since we are aware that we have limited the breadth of our conceptual formulation, we go on to supplement the proposition and the judgment in order to enlarge the contracted scope. We know that we look for the lost breadth, that is, that we look for totality. We started with a dim notion of that totality, which we limited in order to introduce some clarity into its dim character. But we now move towards a totality which will replace the former indistinct breadth with full articulation. Thus the Absolute can be viewed as a result, while it is also the beginning, and it accompanies all the progressive formulations of propositions. That an Absolute as totality accompanies all my propositions – this is one of the possible renderings of Hegel's position. Yet this amounts to asserting that we know the end, that we know what we are seeking, and so we come back, in spite of Hegel, to some of the problems raised by Plato and St. Augustine.

Plato's concept of knowledge based on the notion of recollection (*anamnesis*) actually amounts, as he himself saw, to pre-knowledge. This knowledge lies constantly in the soul, and knowledge proper is an externalization or manifestation of the germinal knowledge in the soul. St. Augustine did not use the concept of recollection, but rather that of the illumination of the soul and the telling of the truth to the soul by God. These are two prominent systems in the history of philosophy which are based on the assumption that knowledge starts from knowledge. The starting point may be recollection of ideas seen before, or may be a sort of whispering by God to the receiving soul. Hegel[22] sees a profound meaning in this concept of recollection, which he expresses as "going to one's inside" (*sich innerlich machen, in sich gehen*).

In spite of Hegel's affinity with the Platonic and Augustinian tradi-

---

[22] *S. W.*, Vol. XVIII, p. 204.

tions on this point, one cannot be oblivious to the fact that with Hegel, the knowledge we start from is redeemed only at the end of the entire process, which is a historical and philosophical process. There is no direct path from the initial knowledge to the sublime knowledge, as is assumed by both Plato and St. Augustine. But as Kosok rightly puts it in dialectical logic, the various terms which are continuously being explicated refer to only one content, so that dialectical knowledge is a continuous re-definition of that which is implicit in the original and initial stage.[23]

To put it otherwise: the aspect of substance is retained in the elevation of substance to the level of subject. Obviously, this connotes that substance is not replaced by subject, nor does subjectivity become a one-sided principle detached from essence and the sum-total of contents. Mere subjectivity would imply nihilism, in the sense introduced into the philosophical vocabulary by Jacobi.[24] The aspect of substance is retained, as the dialectical explication brings about the emergence of knowing, or subject, from the known substance. Moreover, knowing is not merely an attribute of substance; it is its very essence. The known is not parallel to knowing, let alone an external object for knowledge. Knowledge is the explication of the known content, and the known content is implied knowledge. When Hegel, in pointing to the significance of his notions, speaks of a completely different self-consciousness about the truth, it is this self-relation to which he refers. The new self-consciousness is the cornerstone of all actuality, with self-consciousness corresponding to the position of subject, and that which the self-consciousness is about corresponding to the position of substance. A comment should be inserted here about Hegel and Kant with regard to ethical theory. The stress laid on subject as being the ultimate explication of substance has its manifestation in the domain of ethics. If we separate subjectivity from substance, we are bound to follow the line of a subjective ethics, an ethics of what Kant calls "Gesinnungen." For Hegel, subjectivity may deteriorate into a morality of personal particularities. To counteract this detached subjectivity, Hegel tries continuously to synthesize substance and subject – content and awareness, community and individual, social institutions and personal attitudes. The increasingly comprehensive

[23] Michael Kosok, "The Formalization of Hegel's Dialectical Logic" in: *International Philosophical Quarterly* VI, 1966, p. 619.
[24] On Nihilism consult: Otto Pöggeler, "Hegel und die Anfänge der Nihilismus-Diskussion" in: *Man and World*, Vol. 3, No. 3, 4; Sept. – Nov. 1970.

interaction between substance and subject enables Hegel to integrate into his sytem the institutional components of human life, which offers a further vindication of his rendering of the objective as organized, as opposed to the objective as a mere imperative in Kant's sense.[25]

The above analysis shows forth substance turned into subject. This development takes place dialectically, every dialectical stage being a formulation of accompanied by awareness of the achievement expressed in that formulation, as well as of its shortcomings. Reflection cannot be erased. The subject is a reflecting subject comprehending the position at which it has arrived, and the process by which it arrived. Some of the problems dealt with in the course of the present analysis reappear in Hegel's notion of Spirit, and receive there additional development.

A textual comment concerning the present line of interpretation is called for. We took our motif from Hegel's *Phenomenology*, where the shift from substance to subject forms the very program. As is well known, the relationship between the *Phenomenology* and the mature system is a controversial topic in Hegelian scholarship. On this issue, as on many other issues, it seems to be both warranted and advisable to follow the immediate disciples of Hegel, mainly Rosenkranz. These considered the *Phenomenology* to be not only the chronological initiation of the system, but an anticipation of its main notions as well, and, one could add, a treasury of its motifs.[26]

[25] On the basic issues in Hegel's ethical controversy with Kant consult: Joachim Ritter, "Moralität und Sittlichkeit, zu Hegels Auseinandersetzung mit der Kantschen Ethik," included in: *Metaphysik und Politik*, Studien zu Aristoteles und Hegel, Frankfurt a/M 1969, pp. 281ff.

[26] Among contemporary interpreters Otto Pöggeler explicitly refers in hisan alysis to that of Rosenkranz; see his "Zu Deutungen der Phänomenologie des Geistes" included in: *Hegel-Studien I*, 1961. Compare his: "Die Komposition der Phänomenologie des Geistes" included in *Hegel-Studien*, Beiheft 3, 1966. See also Kenley R. Dove, "Hegel's Phenomenological Method" in: *Review of Metaphysics* vol. XXIII, No. 4, June 1970).

# CHAPTER THREE

# POTENTIALITY AND ACTUALITY

## I

In the preceding analysis we were concerned with the concept of subject and the position of the Absolute. We shall now explore the notions of Reason and Spirit and attempt to throw additional light on the issues explored before.

Evolvement from substance to subject brings about the articulation of the structure of the world. The world is identical with Reason – and this again is the meaning of the position of subject in the system. Spirit as a pivotal concept brings into relief the actualization of Reason, Reason in turn inhering in subject. We may even look at the actualization of Reason in Spirit as parallel to the actualization of substance in subject. Yet it is difficult to find in the text explicit evidence for this parallelism.

On one rather significant point the proposed parallelism breaks down. Subject is the realization of the potentialities inherent in substance. Hegel develops this argument by revealing the deficiencies in the category of substance which is caught in the duality of substrate and qualities. No duality can be found in Reason; hence the shift from potentiality to actuality implied in the shift from Reason to Spirit does not involve an overcoming the defect of an alleged duality in Reason. The concept of Idea will serve as the dynamic middle concept between the concepts of Reason and Spirit.

## 2

Reason is consciousness' certainty of being total actuality.[1] Two main features of Reason emerge from this statement: first, Reason is rooted

---

[1] *Phänomenologie*, p. 156.

in consciousness: second, Reason is more than consciousness. It is consciousness whose knowledge is specifically focused on its being all that is actual. Reason is not *Vernunft*, in Kant's sense of the knowledge of principles a priori but rather knowledge of the identity of consciousness and reality. But the identity of consciousness and reality is not confined to Reason in the narrow sense of the term. It applies also to Idea and Spirit, which are related to Reason but lead beyond it in further elaboration of what is inherent in its nature.

As already indicated, Hegel's own description of the nature of Reason, Idea and Spirit does not lack a certain ambiguity as to the definite distinction between them. Their affinity is more visible than their difference. We can suggest the following: Reason is the *potential* identity between consciousness and actuality, while *Spirit* is that same identity as it becomes or has become *actual*. Spirit is Reason at its fullest, while Reason is Spirit in its initial stage. The development from Reason to Spirit goes through the stage of Idea. Idea is the unity of the subjective with the objective, the unity of the two poles which appear in the definition of Reason – consciousness and actuality.[2]

Every actuality is rational, therefore every actuality is an Idea. Thus, Idea is the adequate concept, being the unity of concept and its actuality. A concept which lacks this unity is not adequate, but only an external reflection. As the concept becomes actual it acquires adequate shape and meaning. Only identity provides the full adequacy implied in the notion of truth.[3] Since both Reason and Idea connote identity between concept and reality, there is identity or synonymity, as Hegel has it, of the two terms.

3

Yet in spite of identity or synonymity, there is still a difference between Reason and Idea. The notion of Idea represents a certain dialectical progress *vis-à-vis* the notion of Reason. While Reason is *consciousness*, Idea is *concept*, i.e. it adds to Reason as mere Reason a definite content – that of actuality as identical with concept. Idea is not only the intentionality or activity of cognition in general, but it is that activity focused and made articulate in contents. In other words: within the domain of Reason proper, identity between the subjective and the objective is identity in the domain of awareness, while within

[2] *S. W.*, III, p. 116.
[3] *Logik*, II, p. 505, (II, p. 458); *S. W.*, III, pp. 111, 188.

the domain of Idea this identity progresses to the level of content, besides and in addition to mere awareness.

However, this progress from mere intentionality to a particular noema in terms of actuality and its identity with consciousness is not free from a certain shortcoming. Idea does not carry within itself consciousness of identity with Reason. Identity is there, but initially there is no awareness of it. It is from this point of view that we speak about the ideational character of Nature, Nature being Idea in its otherness. In this position, Nature lacks awareness of itself as Reason. On the level of Reason there is awareness of identity but not in its developed stage i.e. as endowed with specific contents; on the level of Idea there are contents as such identical with Reason, but not necessarily aware of their position and grounding. Spirit embraces thus both specific and defined concepts as well as their self-understood grounding in Reason.[4]

If this interpretation is correct, it may explain why, in the context of history, Hegel distinguishes between Idea and Spirit. The Greek world, for instance, reached the level of Idea, but only the Christian and German world reached the level of thought and its manifestation as Spirit.[5] The distinction between Idea and Spirit implies that Idea is a lower stage in the self-development of Reason to actuality; Plato and Kant considered Idea to be abstract, general, moveless.[6] Ideas may be referred to as abstract, but "abstract Spirit" is a contradiction in terms.

An additional difference between Idea and Reason emerges out of the inner logic of Hegel's system: Idea manifests itself in different spheres. It appears e.g. as the ethical Idea, as the pure Idea in Logic, as the actuality of the ethical Idea in the State, etc. Precisely because the emphasis in the notion of Idea is on contents, the contents provide for a variety of spheres. The realm of Idea is the realm of partiality which has again to be unified in totality. Reason is already totality, just as it is actuality. The route to full realization of totality takes in partial manifestations of Idea and partial modes of consciousness as partial contents. The totality of Reason goes through the partiality of Idea, through the various expressions of Spirit – as subjective, objective and absolute – until it reaches, as Absolute Spirit, full actualization of its initial totality. Partial manifestations reveal the gap between partiality and

---

[4] *Encykl.* § 380.
[5] *S. W.*, XVII, p. 136.
[6] *Ibid.*, 516, 574.

totality, creating momentum toward the totality. This is the full swing from Reason to Spirit, corresponding to the swing from being to concept, or to that from substance to subject.

4

Moving now from this – as it were – topographical delineation of the notion of Spirit to some of its more concrete features, we enumerate the following:

(a) Spirit is fundamentally reflection. Obviously this trait is an aspect of the element of consciousness inherent in the nature of Reason. Thought is understood as an activity setting for itself its own content, and this is probably Hegel's interpretation of the spontaneous character of thought.[7] But the activity which creates its own content is an activity which turns towards itself; it is reflection precisely because it is spontaneous. Only Spirit as such, says Hegel, knows that its nature is Reason and truth, truth, again, being identity between thought and actuality.[8]

Here the step is taken which carries the system beyond the level of Idea: Spirit, both content and consciousness, points toward identity. Furthermore, this notion exhibits the systematic position of philosophy. Spirit is reflection as awareness of the content of Reason which becomes actual, as well as reflection as identity of actuality with Reason. As we move from Reason to Spirit, placing on the level of Absolute Spirit the full actuality known by full knowledge, a system of reflection of reflection takes shape, i.e., philosophy. We move from (1) Reason to Idea as the development of the content inherent in Reason, to (2) Spirit which knows Reason and its content, to (3) philosophy which knows Spirit along with the entire process leading to it.

(b) Spirit is fundamentally activity. The active character of Spirit is its thinking character. The relationship between Spirit and Reason is analogous to the relationship between body and weight, or will and freedom. Spirit as the active manifestation of Reason is likened to body which is the active manifestation, or let us say, embodiment, of weight, and to will which is the active expression and actualization of freedom. Body is concealed within weight as will is inherent in freedom.[9] Spirit is both the process and the order created by the process. And in clear

---

[7] *S. W.*, III, p. 113.
[8] *Encykl.* Zusatz, § 387.
[9] *Encykl.* Zusatz 387.

parallel to substance and subject, the relation between Reason and Spirit retains the process leading to the order, making them ultimately identical, as for instance, the history of philosophy is identical with the whole of philosophy.

We have here a kind of supra-metaphysical guiding principle in Hegel: though totality is the origin, it is only through the process that it becomes what it is; and to be the totality is to be impregnated with knowledge. Then there is the process, the continuous mediation between totality as the beginning and totality as the end. Within the process there are stages of increasing actualization, which means that there are also realms of Spirit as stages of the process. There is Subjective Spirit, Objective Spirit and Absolute Spirit. Only Absolute Spirit is what Spirit essentially is, namely Reason identical with actuality and knowing that identity and that actuality. There is in Hegel a kind of rhythm of deferred actualization. But this deferment comes to an end in the categories and in Spirit. As opposed to Neo-Platonism where the activity of mind is one of emanation from the higher level to the lower, in Hegel the activity of Spirit is one of elevation from the lower level to the higher one.

Since Spirit is essentially an activity and since that activity is teleological in character, leading to the full realization of Reason, the difference between intellect and will disappears. "The distinction between thought and will is only that between the theoretical attitude and the practical. These, however, are surely not two faculties. The will is rather a special way of thinking, thinking translating itself into existence, thinking as the urge to give itself existence."[10] Since Spirit is understood as a creative activity, there is no need to turn to will as a special activity different from thinking. Thus there is established through the concept of Spirit the "Primacy" of Theoretical Reason, which absorbs in itself the practical-creative Reason. Hegel's concept of freedom, which will be explored in the next chapter, is grounded here.

In this context, we should notice in connection with freedom that in spite of creativity in history, institutions and world-outlooks, this creativity remains within its own boundaries and does not posit objects detached from itself. Every strangeness becomes transparent because on the level of Spirit, where there is full identity between Reason and actuality, there is no strangeness.

---

[10] Hegel's *Philosophy of Right*, translated with notes by T. M. Knox, Oxford 1942 p. 226.

(c) Spirit is unity. Precisely because Spirit transcends mere consciousness and creates actuality, it connotes the unity between the creation of actuality and the actuality created. In creation, an alienation or self-alienation takes place, because creation is expressed in an order or system. But on the level of Spirit self-identity is regained. Spirit is that which keeps its identity in its otherness.[11]

(d) Spirit is concreteness. The absolutely most concrete element is Spirit,[12] where concrete, according to Hegel, denotes unity of different determinations. This unity, too, is achieved on the level of Spirit. Hegel's disciple Erdmann described philosophical speculation as the intellectual re-statement of concreteness: speculation creates its own self-reflection in the world; speculation as philosophical activity proper reflects the activity of Spirit as self-reflection in the world.[13] Paraphrasing a well-known saying about the soul being essentially Christian we may express this notion as follows: *mundus naturaliter philosophicus, ergo anima naturaliter philosophica*.

Summing up we may say that Spirit is both the instrument of Reason's realization leading towards actuality as well as the outcome of the process of that realization. In all of its features, we place Spirit *vis-à-vis* Reason in a position parallel to that of subject *vis-à-vis* consciousness. Spirit is one of the notions which indicates the character of Hegel's dialectic of fullness becoming articulate fullness. New elements are not acquired; latent or inherent ones are expressed. The only transition within the sphere of fullness is that from opaqueness to self-consciousness.

5

A historical comment should supplement this analysis. As the shift from substance to subject represents a kind of synthesis of Spinoza and Kant, the shift from Reason to Spirit represents a kind of synthesis of Aristotle and Descartes.

The distinction between potentiality and actuality, a distinction within the domain of fullness, is for Hegel a primordial, axiomatic one. These two aspects are to be traced even in the realm of thinking. Reason is potentiality in the domain of thinking while in that same domain, Spirit is actuality. Yet actuality is not brought about by a

---

[11] *Phänomenologie* p. 518.
[12] *Encykl.* § 164.
[13] J. E. Erdmann, *Psychologische Briefe*,[2] Leipzig 1856, p. 331.

factor that existed formerly and formally outside the potentiality and giving shape to potentiality considered as matter. Actuality is brought about by the potentiality itself. Potentiality in Hegel's sense is an active repository of content and an activity of self-transcendence in order to find itself in the other. Reason as potentiality creates Spirit as its own actuality, which actuality is realized in and through Spirit.[14]

On the other hand, Hegel starts off with the Cartesian notion of reflection as an index of itself as well as an index of existence. Descartes confines the existential aspect of reflection to the *sum cogitans*. Hegel enlarges, as it were, the scope of reflection. For him, reflection is a fundamental feature of actuality as totality and not only a feature of the *cogito* as an Ego. Not only the Ego reflects on itself, but the universe at large reflects on itself. This enlarged reflection is contained in the notion of Spirit. Subject absorbs object, while object is transformed into subject. The enlarged Ego of Descartes brings Hegel back to Aristotle, for whom supreme thinking is the thinking of thinking itself. Here is the root of Hegel's identification of Spirit with God.[15]

The entire system appears here as a projection of reflection outside the confined or limited consciousness. The system is a philosophical world-outlook that regards the world as an incarnation of consciousness in the world. This view of the world will be dealt with later in an analysis of Hegel's view of philosophy.

6

We started off our analysis of the relation of Reason and Spirit by pointing out that Hegel's text is not always univocal or helpful in revealing the structural relationship between these two notions. Rosenkranz's statement seems to be more helpful on that score. Spirit, he says, *is* only *what it does*. It is, therefore, to be conceived only as development.[16] If our reading of Rosenkranz is correct, this corrob-

---

[14] On the concept of Spirit consult: a. J. N. Findlay, *Hegel: A Re-Examination*, New York, 1962, pp. 31ff. b. Emil L. Fackenheim, *The Religious Dimension In Hegel's Thought*, Bloomington & London, 1967, pp. 18ff, 108–109.

[15] Pöggeler points in this context to the Aristotelian notion of life as identical with self-moving, and he suggests that this notion runs counter to the Cartesian *cogito*. Yet it appears that in spite of this antithetic aspect emphasized by Pöggeler's interpretation, the attempted synthesis of Aristotle and Descartes cannot be overlooked. Otto Pöggeler, "Die Komposition der Phänomenologie des Geistes" in *Hegel-Studien*, Beiheft 3, 1966, p. 56.

[16] Karl Rosenkranz, *Psychologie, oder Wissenschaft vom subjektiven Geist*, Königsberg 1837, p. 226.

orates what we have seen to be the case with the concept of Spirit in general, that the emphasis is on doing, on actualization. In his presentation, doing amounts to development, the latter connoting not only conceptual explication but also temporal process – and this indeed is a recurrent theme in the system and its variations.

As to the relation between Spirit proper and Reason proper, Rosenkranz observes that one cannot think of Spirit without Reason. He attempts to allocate to Reason a function in the scope of Spirit, but does not assume an identity between them. Reason, as he puts it, is an absolute organ of Spirit. There is a proximity between Spirit and Reason, but that proximity does not lead to identity. Identity is rather found within Spirit proper, which is its own concept as well as its own content.[17] We may paraphrase this by saying that Spirit is both content and organ, while Reason is organ only.

The process of actualization of Spirit and the possible employment of Reason as an organ in that process is epitomized in the various spheres of development. The most prominent illustration of development is religion. In the development of religions we find both a progressive articulation of the hidden content of religion as well as the delineation of their forms occurring in historical time. But precisely this actualization and process bring us back to the distinction between substance and subject and their ultimate unification and reconciliation. The absolute religion, which is in Hegel's system Christianity, contains the subjective determination of the infinite form which conforms (*gleich ist*) to substance.[18] In the history of religion there is a growing intensification and explication of the identity of substance and subject. This identity is the *telos* of the development of religions, leading to Christianity – and this explains why in Hegel's view Christianity is Religion of Spirit proper. Thus, even the concept of Idea does not adequately explicate the exhibition of universal substance as subject, and we are bound to employ the notion of Spirit.

Here again Rosenkranz sheds light on the issue both as a commentator and as a follower of the system and its trend. About religions he says that they indeed differ very much one from the other, yet they are identical in that they posit (*setzen*) God as the absolute substance. Christianity is grounded in the proposition that God is Man; substance is in itself and for itself subject.[19] Thus, the position of Christianity

17 *Idem* p. 222.
18 *S. W.*, XVI, p. 197.
19 Karl Rosenkranz, *System der Wissenschaft, ein philosophisches Encheiridion*, Königsberg, 1850, p. 575, p. 587.

finds its categorial equivalent in the convergence of substance and subject, and its absolute and consummating position in the sequence of the history of religions is vindicated.

Spirit is in Hegel the sphere of actuality and actualization, actualization having, as it were, its *causa materialis* in substance and its *causa formalis* and *finalis* in subject. Since Spirit is the realm of activity and expression, the analysis of the position of Spirit leads us to the exploration of the concept of freedom.

# CHAPTER FOUR

## NECESSITY AND FREEDOM

I

Progress toward perfection in Hegel is progress within the closed circuit of the evolvement from totality to totality – this is in a way the outcome of our previous analysis. The given totality with which we start can be viewed as accidental, while the achieved totality has to be viewed as necessary. Yet this necessity is not one of circumstances which we have to take for granted. It is a cognitively transparent necessity which has ceased to be an imposition and has become a self-regulated actuality. On the level of the articulated totality the distinction between necessity and freedom is sublated, just as the distinction between Reason and Idea is sublated on the level of Spirit. Mere necessity exists only before the achievement of adequacy with the concept. On the level of Spirit mere necessity is replaced by the synthesis of necessity and freedom.

Our endeavor now will be to throw some light on Hegel's notion of freedom, including the notion of political freedom. We shall proceed by way of a comparison between the concept of freedom in Kant and the concept of freedom in Hegel, both for the sake of the analysis of Hegel's concept, and in order to place it in a proper light and perspective.

2

Kant distinguishes between the cosmological aspect of the concept of freedom, and the practical one which is based on the transcendental idea of cosmological freedom.[1]

Freedom in the cosmological sense is the capacity of starting a state

---

[1] *Kr. d. r. V.*, B 561 (Kemp Smith's trans. 464) As indicated before the references in brackets refer to that translation.

of affairs out of itself. Causality of this state of affairs is not by way of conformity with the law of nature. It is timeless and independent of sensible factors:[2] the start of a state of affairs *ab initio* cannot occur in time. Were it to occur in time, it would be related to a previous state of affairs in time and could not, therefore, be a start contained in itself. Its independence from time puts freedom on the level of Reason, and thus on the level of a transcendental or cosmological idea. Cosmological ideas or concepts of the world connote, in this context, ideas referring to the unconditioned.[3] All these descriptions of the cosmological meaning of the idea of freedom are, as a matter of fact, synonymous; the unconditioned means only that which necessarily drives us beyond the limits of experience and phenomena.[4]

Freedom in the practical sense is, in a way, just a specification of freedom in the cosmological sense. Cosmological freedom implies independence from the conditions of the world of sense, while practical freedom implies independence of the will with regard to determination by human sensibility.[5] Practical freedom functions within the closer empirical context of human sensibility and not only within the broad context of the conditions of sensibility *qua* time and space. Freedom in this sense is not the state of affairs initiating itself in general, but the exercise of will or choice, what Kant sometimes defines as *Willkür*, *arbitrium liberum* as distinguished from *arbitrium brutum*.[6]

The relationship of practical and cosmological freedom can also be expressed this way: "With the pure practical faculty of reason, the reality of transcendental freedom is also confirmed ... This idea is revealed by the moral law."[7] The revelation of the idea by the moral law illumines the position of Reason within the domain of practical freedom. Practical freedom is that freedom in which Reason has causality, i.e., causative impact, according to motives objectively determined, by Reason itself.[8] Reason as such is free and cannot be determined by sensibility. In practical freedom, Reason becomes a causality, thus realizing its fundamental spontaneity. Man can determine himself by principles of Reason, so that a human deed can be

---

[2] *Ibid.*, 567 (468).
[3] *Ibid.*, 710 (557).
[4] *Ibid.*, 435 (386).
[5] *Ibid.*, 561 (446).
[6] *Ibid.*, 562, 830 (465, 633).
[7] *Kritik der praktischen Vernunft*, ed. K. Vorländer (Leipzig 1929), pp. 3–4 (in L. White Beck's trans., New York, 1956, pp. 3–4).
[8] *Prolegomena zu einer jeden künftigen Metaphysik die als Wissenschaft wird auftreten können*, § 53.

looked upon as free from the point of view of its intelligible cause. At the same time it is a phenomenon to be looked at as empirically conditioned.[9]

It should be noticed at this juncture that there are at least two connotations in Kant's usage of the term causality (*Kausalität*). First, causality is a principle, that is to say a rule of succession in time, or else a rule according to which all changes occur in conformity with the law of the connection of cause and effect.[10] This usage is neither fully clear nor consistent, since causality has another connotation as well: Second, causality connotes the character of the cause in so far as it produces the effect.[11] When Kant speaks, for example, about freedom being the unconditioned causality of the cause of a phenomenon, or about the true causality of Reason, he does not refer to the *rule* of causality but to the capacity of freedom to be both productive cause and rule. This is absolute spontaneity of cause or absolute spontaneity of activity.[12] It is in this sense that the *Critique of Practical Reason* deals with the notion of causality – the causality of freedom.

The question arises: How is Reason productive also of a rule? We may suggest that in practical freedom, the component of will provides for the productive aspect of causality, while the component of Reason provides for the aspect of rule or universal law. Let us comment on this and see how it brings out Kant's notion of autonomy.

Will can be viewed generically as the motor of action; it is the sponsoring factor of a decision to perform an action or to act in a certain direction. Will can thus be understood as the producing component in a deed. As against this, Reason can be viewed as the sum total of to-be-known-principles guiding the action and giving it meaning, direction or validity. In Kant's own words: "a being which is capable of actions by the idea of laws is an intelligence (a rational being), and the causality of such a being according to this idea of laws is his will."[13] Then the idea of freedom as a faculty of absolute spontaneity combines will and Reason: spontaneity is systematically related

---

[9] B 564 (466); *Prolegomena*, § 53.
[10] *B* 246, 183, 232 (226, 184, 217).
[11] *Prolegomena*, § 53.
[12] *B* 474 (429).
[13] The difference between Reason and will as expressed here is paralleled by other statements of Kant. He speaks about Reason as concerned with grounds determining the will, while will is a faculty either of bringing forth objects corresponding to representations, or of determining itself. Will is causal with regard to such objects; Reason as the faculty of principles is distinguished from the will's power of determination. *Kritik der pr. Ver.* 144 (Lewis White Beck's transl. 130). Consult also: 16, 138; (transl. 15, 124).

to Reason or to thinking, but right here, one of its characteristics is that it produces representations or concepts out of itself.[14] The productive aspect of freedom arises from the engendering characteristic of will. Thinking as such is spontaneity;[15] freedom as such is spontaneity too.[16]

The law of Reason is the determining ground of the will, and it is the property of the will to be its own law. Will, here, implies independence of sensibility, which independence places it in relation to the law; or else, autonomy lies in perpetuation of the will in its independence of sensibility.[17] Independence from sensibility, the negative aspect of freedom, is by the same token self-legislation, the positive aspect of will.[18]

In this theory of freedom as productive cause containing the guiding rule within itself, i.e., freedom as will and Reason, Kant brings about a sort of synthesis between the voluntary and intellectual theories of freedom found in the philosophy of the Middle Ages, namely, that Reason is the *supremus motor* of psychic life, or – the second position – that will is *movens per se*. The voluntary ingredient is retained in the theory of will as producing action; the intellectual ingredient is retained inasmuch as the rule of Reason makes will not only independent of nature but positively a cause.

This move toward the synthesis of will and Reason shaped Kant's whole theory of freedom. It has social and political consequences, as can be seen in his adherence to the theory of social contract.

## 3

We have already referred to the distinction between *arbitrium brutum* and *arbitrium liberum*; the former is a choice dictated by sensible drives while the latter is one determined by Reason. This distinction underlies again Kant's adherence to the theory of social contract which echoes some of the fundamental ideas of Rousseau.

As citizen of a state – Kant insists – man does not give up his innate freedom for the sake of an end; he leaves behind only a wild, lawless freedom in order to find his freedom in a lawful state of affairs without

[14] B 75, 93 (93, 105).
[15] B 428 (381).
[16] B 446, 476 (392, 412).
[17] *Kritik der praktischen Vernunft*, p. 51 (L. White Beck, p. 44).
[18] *Grundlegung zur Metaphysik der Sitten*, in: *Kants gesammelte Schriften*, ed. Königliche Preussische Akademie der Wissenschaften, vol. IV (Berlin 1911) pp. 446ff.

any diminution whatever. Man finds freedom in its entirety in the state, since his dependence upon the state and its "state of affairs" emerges out of his own legislative will.[19] It is clear (a) that the wild will corresponds to *arbitrium brutum*; (b) that freedom in the state corresponds to *arbitrium liberum*; and (c) that the idea of self-legislation as manifestation and safeguard of freedom is but a translation and amplification in the political sphere of the idea of ethical autonomy. The original contract is an implementation of the idea of autonomy or else it is autonomy written large. The greatest problem for the human race, a problem which nature forces man to resolve, is the achievement of a civil society (*bürgerliche Gesellschaft*). A civil society is one in which freedom under external law is compatible with power.[20] To achieve such a state, the necessary first step lies in the act of freedom establishing an order which preserves freedom. Social contract presupposes freedom and comes about for the sake of freedom.

Kant's systematic interpretation – in this case we may say: proviso – of the term "idea" as a concept which goes beyond the possibility of experience and pertains to Reason alone, comes to his aid in solving the notorious question as to whether the contract is a historical fact or only a conceptual supposition. This contract, he says, is not a fact and is not possible as a fact. It is a mere idea of Reason which, just the same, has its (practical) reality.[21]

We may sum up by saying that the idea of an original social contract is a continuation of the idea of freedom in its practical sense, or else, the orbit of social and political life is a practical realization of the fundamental idea of freedom. In the concept of social contract we find again the interrelation between will and Reason. The addition of the notion of social contract to the basic meaning of freedom is related essentially to the question of context for both of them. The categorical imperative in its primary formulation refers to man but not to the plurality of persons. This plurality, in turn, is the extension of the realization of the notion of man implied in the categorical imperative. The state is based on the idea of social contract. The latter, being based on the notion of autonomy, is a realization of the "ethical idea" taken here in Kant's sense and not in the sense of his critical successor.

---

[19] *Metaphysik der Sitten*, § 47.
[20] *Geschichte in weltbürgerlicher Absicht*, 5. Satz.
[21] *Über den Gemeinspruch: das mag in der Theorie richtig sein, taugt aber nicht für die Praxis, Sämmtliche Werke*, ed. Vorländer, Vol. VI, Leipzig 1922, p. 92.

4

A comment on Spinoza is necessary before we proceed to the concept of freedom in Hegel. Spinoza deals with will, distinguishing clearly between will and choice. He also has a notion of social contract, with reference to which he places choice and will, although these are of a different order than that of will when it faces clear and distinct ideas:

... By the will to affirm and decide, I mean the faculty, not the desire ... the faculty, whereby the mind affirms or denies what is true or false, not the desire, wherewith the mind wishes for or turns away from any given thing.[22]

There is in the mind no volition or affirmation and negation, save that which an idea, inasmuch as it is an idea, involves.[23]

... This idea of a triangle must involve this same affirmation, namely, that its three interior angles are equal to two right angles ... This affirmation belongs to the essence of the idea of a triangle, and is nothing besides.[24]

From this the corollary:

Will and understanding are one and the same.[25]

We have to distinguish desire or appetite from will proper as the confirmation or denial of truth. Desire and appetite are related to the drive to preserve man's existence and not to the conception of ideas and truths. Will as affirmation of truth cannot be free since it is determined by the truth it affirms. Will is not a motivating cause but provides consent to that which by its very character as true calls for consent. In other words, will activates man's grasp of a truth. But this active component in man is a correlate of truth, not a motivation to decide or choose concerning the content of the truth. Kant in turn tried to combine decision with that which ought to be decided for. In Spinoza, will is an activity of confirmation, not a momentum of decision. Hence there is not practical Reason but will, or, Reason which is identical with will. In Kant there is a tacit circular argumentation: to be free is to be emancipated from the wild will and to opt for the good will. But this very option for the good will can be brought about only by the good will itself, that is to say, by an act of giving preference to the universal direction provided by Reason over particularist desire, i.e. the factual drives of man. The direction of the will, in

---

[22] *The Chief Works of Benedict de Spinoza*, tr. R. H. M. Elwes (New York 1951), Vol. II, p. 120.

[23] *Ibid.*

[24] *Ibid.*

[25] *Ibid.*

Spinoza, is not a decision of the will; it is provided by the content which determines the will and calls for the confirmation of that content. To be sure, will is present, since the intellectual confirmation, though called for by the content – the triangle in the example – is not identical with the triangle. The confirmation is caused ideally by the content but is not really or effectually engendered by it.

Desire and appetite, in turn, are related not to the idea or to the truth but to the preservation of human nature:

> There are ... many things outside ourselves, which are useful to us, and are, therefore, to be desired. Of such none can be discerned more excellent, than those which are in entire agreement with our nature ... To man there is nothing more useful than man.[26]

Desire, and not will proper, is at the source of the social contract establishing the state. Will is totally out of place here, since we are not in the sphere of correlation with truth, but within the sphere of the desire to exist:

> ... The ultimate aim of government is not to rule, or restrain by fear, nor to exact obedience, but contrariwise, to free every man from fear, that he may live in all possible security; in other words, to strengthen his natural right to exist and work without injury to himself or others.[27]

When Spinoza speaks, in the context of the social contract, about dictates of reason, he relates these dictates to their utility for men. There is thus a systematic correlation between will versus truth on the one hand, and desire versus reason (as prudence) on the other, reason providing the means for the implementation of desire. The social contract is a means of – the state – to be viewed from the angle of utility. Here lies the explanation of Spinoza's statement that "reason ... is always on the side of peace ... and the more a man is led by reason ... the more constantly will he respect the laws of his country ..."[28]

Thus, the social contract is not treated within the context of the realization of freedom, as an extension of the autonomy of man and the realization of *arbitrium liberum*. In Spinoza, it is to be placed in the sphere which Kant calls technical as distinct from practical – technical being the orbit of a possible action which is able to bring about a certain effect, while practical delineates the sphere where will is de-

---

[26] *Ibid.*, p. 201.
[27] *A Theologico-Political Treatise, ibid.*, vol. I, pp. 258–259.
[28] *Ibid.*, p. 276.

termined by a principle. The practical, we may add, is inherently related to the will, as the categorical imperative is, and vice versa. We may sum up by saying:

(a) In Kant, there is combination of will and choice; in Spinoza, there is separation of will and choice, that is to say, where there is will there is no choice, and where there is choice there is no will. In Spinoza, will is the correlate of adequate knowledge and not a motive for action.

(b) Where there is a motive for action there is desire, and search for useful means to safeguard the source of the desire, i.e., human nature.

(c) The social contract arises from man's search for means of subsistence, and not from man's realizing practically the practical idea of freedom.

(d) Where there is full rationality there is no choice; this is Spinoza's view. Where there is full spontaneity of Reason there is, by the same token, choice; this is Kant's view. For Spinoza, choice means execution of the dictates of the desire; for Kant, choice is precisely that which lifts men up from brutality to human – practical, free – status.

(e) Spinoza has two concepts of will, will as consent and will as desire, and also two concepts of rationality, rationality as the domain of truth and rationality as the domain of usefulness.

(f) The state is for Spinoza an instrument within the domain of instrumentality; for Kant, it is a realization of the idea of freedom as the practical idea.

Thus, both Spinoza and Kant adhere to the notion of social contract, each for different reasons. Kant abolished, in a way, the systematic difference between the two wills, retaining will as appetite, or *arbitrium brutum* on the psychological level, and denying its significance on the ethical level. He establishes the continuity from will to action and to the state, the social contract being primarily an act of will in his own sense. Hegel set out to abolish in his own way the distinctions Kant had retained, and the controversies which ensued from them.[29]

## 5

There is an innocent word in the German vocabulary – *Willkür*. Its literal meaning is action accomplished upon free choice. The derivative

[29] Consult H. A. Wolfson, *The Philosophy of Spinoza* (New York 1958), vol. I, pp. 164ff.

*willkürlich* connotes *freiwillig*, in the sense of "arbitrary." In turning this word into a philosophical term, Kant was not always consistent. Sometimes he speaks about *Willkür* as will in general, distinguishing within this broad scope between sensible *Willkür*, and free *Willkür* as synonymous with freedom of will as absolute spontaneity.[30] In this sense, *Willkür* as determined by pure Reason is called free will. To the extent that will implies arbitrariness (in the sense of a "willful" deed), *Willkür* connotes that which is not done according to a maxim of Reason. It is arbitrary, but not free in the sense of being determined by Reason.

Hegel, like Kant, oscillates with respect to the connotations of this word. *Willkür* is freedom inasmuch as the will refers to something limited[31] – the limited is the opposite of the total or universal as well as of that which belongs to the realm of Reason proper. Again, close to Kant in his usage of *Willkür* as sensible will, Hegel speaks of *Willkür* as a choice between inclinations, i.e., as a choice not sponsored by "the Reason of the will."[32]

Hegel went a step further: what was, for Kant, freedom proper – spontaneous choice determined by Reason, is placed by Hegel also as *Willkür*. Freedom in Kant's sense is in Hegel's eyes only abstract freedom, formal freedom, an empty opinion about freedom.[33] Abstract freedom is opposed to necessity and does not include necessity in itself. It is here that we find the main difference between Hegel and Kant in their interpretations of will and freedom and in their use of the shifting meaning of the term *Willkür*. As against what might be described as an antithetic concept of freedom where freedom is the opposite of necessity, we find in Hegel what might be described as a totalistic concept of freedom, i.e., freedom including necessity. This may be seen in the light of the relation between freedom and necessity in Spinoza. We read in the *Ethics*:

That thing is called free, which exists solely by the necessity of its own nature, and of which the action is determined by itself alone. On the other hand, that thing is necessary, or rather constrained, which is determined by something external to itself to a fixed and definite method of existence or action.[34]

God acts solely by the laws of His own nature, and is not constrained by anyone.[35]

[30] B p. 830 (653).
[31] *S. W.*, III, p. 47.
[32] *S. W.*, XII, p. 144.
[33] *S. W.*, XVIII, p. 55.
[34] *Ed. Cit.*, II, p. 46.
[35] *Ibid.*, p. 59.

According to Spinoza, freedom is found where the motive for action follows the immanent necessity of the agent, while constraint is the subjugation to the external causality. Spinoza does not see a diametric opposition between necessity and freedom, since he understands necessity as the inner structure of the substance which is the agent, resulting in a certain course prescribed by that inner structure. As against this it emerges that Kant's concept of necessity, as confined to the sphere of possible experience, cannot permit an absolute necessity as a reality because it would, in his system, stem from mere concepts.[36] He deals with necessity as it is related to causality, not to the immanent nature or the structure of a substance. Necessity bears on the connection between the reality of one thing and the reality of another. It is a necessity of "*gesetzt werden*,"[37] not bearing on substance in the comprehensive sense of the term, i.e., subject. Since for Kant freedom means the capacity to start a state of affairs out of itself, that capacity is synonymous with spontaneity. In this sense freedom is opposed to, and is not an emanation of, necessity.

Necessity as understood by Kant is, for Hegel, a relative or accidental necessity.[38] According to this inferior and limited sense, the result is necessary, while the circumstances – i.e., the conditions – are accidental or contingent. The conditioning causes differ from the results.[39] A higher form of necessity is centered in the direction of process: result and presupposition are distinct only in terms of form.[40] The causal relation in time cannot exemplify inner necessity. A proper example of intrinsic necessity would be the relationship between the infinite and the finite. They are not mutually exclusive. They are only determinations or moments of the selfsame process. Neither the finite as such is the being, nor is the infinite as such the being. God is finite, just as the Ego is infinite.[41] Another example of inner necessity would be the unity of the spiritual and the natural: neither is exclusive, each one is related – through alienation – with the other.[42] We come back here to the relation between substance and subject, or between potentiality and actuality – while these different pairs of concept take on now the meaning of the distinction between necessity and freedom.

---

[36] B 635 (510).
[37] *Prolegomena* § 27.
[38] *S. W.*, XVI, p. 20.
[39] *Ibid.*, p. 21.
[40] *Ibid.*, pp. 21–23.
[41] *S. W.*, XV pp. 210ff.
[42] *Ibid.*, p. 218.

There is a difference here between Spinoza and Hegel: Spinoza stressed, on the one hand, lack of dependence, and on the other, the immanence of the emerging, as being characteristic of freedom, and making freedom eventually identical with necessity. Hegel stresses mutual dependence between the poles as characteristic of inner necessity. We remain in Hegel within the realm of immanence, and this immanence is exhibited in the interdependence of the poles. We do not find in Hegel the linear structure of emergence or deduction which we notice in Spinoza.

There is in Hegel a concept of necessity as absolute necessity. Absolute necessity contains freedom within itself. Process is nothing more than oscillation between poles, e.g., the infinite and the finite of God and the Ego. Process is inner convergence, in which substance finds itself.[43] The process has a *telos*, and not only the rhythm of a mutual positing (*setzen*). The *telos* lies in the self-revelation or else the self-discovery of substance. The turning from substance to subject is related to this concept of necessity, and thus to its correlate or synonym, freedom.

Inner revelation, tantamount to both freedom and necessity, is implied in the notion that freedom is the substance of Spirit.[44] Freedom connotes here what it connoted, formally, both in Spinoza and Kant: negatively, the absence of dependence upon an external factor; positively, relation to itself. Self-contained relation of the Absolute to itself, again a notion of Spinoza, brings about a process or an activity. Spinoza stressed the self-contained character of freedom and necessity; Kant stressed freedom's character as a capacity to start a state of affairs out of one's own causality, i.e., the relation between freedom and activity. Hegel combines these two aspects by stating that the exposition of the Absolute is the latter's own deed. Exposition here is the translation of *auslegen*, which means bringing to an understanding, and is related to the Latin *exponere*, which means to place, to show or to exhibit something for sale. Hegel took over from Spinoza the idea of necessity. Yet since necessity means a lack of constraint, he interpreted necessity as spontaneity, in the sense introduced by Kant. From Kant, Hegel took over the idea of freedom *qua* spontaneity or activity. But since this activity stems from fullness, there is nothing to be created by the activity. It becomes exposition with teleological direction, or self-teleological, i.e., exposition for the sake of the self-understanding

---

43 *S. W.*, XVI, p. 25.
44 *S. W.*, XI, p. 44.

of fullness. Since activity does not create, freedom ceases to be a cause. It becomes a situation. The question of the identity between exposition and activity, which in turn leads to the identity between necessity and freedom, calls for an analysis of the relation between will and thinking, or will and Reason. We thus come back to the distinction analysed before, against the background of the different statements of the identity between totality at the beginning and totality at the end.

6

We recall that for Kant will is the motive while Reason is the determining ground. For Spinoza will is consent to the truth of a statement; it is correlative to Reason. What shape does the relation between will and Reason take in Hegel?

The distinction between thought and will is only that between the theoretical attitude and the practical. These, however, are surely not two faculties; the will is rather a special way of thinking, thinking translating itself into existence, thinking as the urge to give itself existence.[45]

Hegel uses the term "practical" in the conventional sense as an attitude starting from an inner determination and bringing about a state of affairs by way of a deed which originates in that inner determination, direction entertained or decision. The theoretical attitude, again, is taken in the conventional sense as starting from a presently-existent (*ein Daseiendes*) and turning the external into an idea or representation (*Vorstellung*).

How does Hegel, taking as his point of departure this conventional understanding of practical and theoretical, conceive of their identity? He himself explains it this way: In thinking an object, I make it into thought and deprive it of its sensibility. This corresponds to turning the external thing into an idea. But an idea is always universal and to universalize is to think.[46] In the theoretical attitude to the world I make the world a content of my own. The practical attitude, on the other hand, begins in thinking, in the Ego. In so far as I am active, in so far as I do something, I determine myself. When I posit these determinations in the so-called external world, they remain mine. In the theoretical attitude, the world becomes mine; in the practical at-

---

[45] *Hegel's Philosophy of Right*, trans. T. M. Knox (Oxford 1942), p. 226.
[46] *Ibid.*, p. 30.

titude my world becomes the world. From this point of view a process of transition takes place from the Ego to the world. The difference between the two attitudes is just the difference in the direction of the transition.

Hegel goes a step further to assert an inner tie between the two attitudes. Will contains the theoretical component in its practical attitude because whatever I will, I hold before my mind as an idea. Thus the practical is tied to the theoretical because the object of the will is *pari passu* an object of thought. Moreover, because thinking is an activity and activity is the essence of the practical, the theoretical is tied to the practical.[47]

Does this exhaust the relation between will and Reason in Hegel's system, and does it do justice to his intention? In what we have dealt with so far, Hegel has been concerned only with the *relation* between willing and thinking. His intention, however, was to establish the *identity* of thought and will. Let us recall a previous part of our interpretation.

As we have already shown, Spirit (*Geist*) denotes the comprehensive sphere within which transitions take place and where the result is shaped by the transitions and their stages. *Geist* as subjectivity is intelligence, while *Geist* as objectivity is will.[48] The highest command, the essence of Spirit, is to know itself as that which it is, to be aware of itself and to bring itself about (*wissen und hervorbringen*). Knowledge is the essence of Spirit; knowledge itself is the self-explication of Spirit; bringing about a state of affairs is both knowledge and deed.

The conventional description of the theoretical and practical attitudes assumed that there is *prima facie* the world turned into the Ego and the Ego turned into the world. But in Hegel's dialectical view Spirit brings itself about and creates the object out of itself, since the object is but Spirit in its estranged manifestation. Hence the distinction between the Ego and the world ceases to be a distinction between poles and becomes a distinction between transitional steps of the selfsame process. While the conventional distinction between willing and thinking presupposes the distinction between subject and object and, on the basis of this distinction, a connection between will and thinking is sought, the dialectical view takes the split into subject and object to be itself a manifestation of the totality of Spirit. The split is a process or an activity, while reflection or awareness of their

47 *Ibid.*, pp. 226–227.
48 *S. W.*, X, p. 51.

identity is thinking. Thinking and willing are not two sides of the same coin; they are the same coin.

Yet there is an additional ingredient of this argument:

When the will's potentialities have become fully explicit, then it has for its object the will as such, and so the will in its sheer universality ... But this process of absorption in or elevation to universality is what is called the activity of thought.[49]

We can explain this passage according to the idea that in thinking the external is turned into the internal, becoming an idea of the Ego and thus universal. But we can consider the passage from Kant's point of view as well, that the will which opts for the universal rule is will proper, or self-legislative. Autonomy or self-legislation implies universality; universality in turn is the characteristic feature of thinking, thus making universality the *tertium comparationis* between thinking and will. It will also provide for the identity of the two. The universality of Hegel is that of the "universal law" in Kant's sense of the term. Hegel seems to say that the very intentionality to the universal is not a practical intentionality but one where the separation between the practical and the theoretical disappears and the identity between the two is established. Reason is not only the determiner of will, but thinking is identical with will.

There is an unresolved ambiguity in Kant with respect to the relation between will and freedom, and not only with respect to the relation between will and Reason. Kant speaks about the autonomy of the will, autonomy being a specific property of will and not simply identical with it. The will which always conforms to the maxim of the moral law is in all respects good. We have again to distinguish, between will and good will, the latter being eventually free will or freedom.[50] Hegel attempts apparently to remove this residual duality between will and freedom. Freedom is just as fundamental a character of the will as is weight of bodies. We cannot say it is only contingent that matter is "heavy," because nothing material is without weight. Matter is rather weight itself. Heaviness constitutes the body and is the body. The same is the case with freedom and the will, since what is free is the will. "Will without freedom is an empty word, while freedom is actual only as will, as subject."[51] Hegel is lead to identify freedom

---

[49] *Hegel's Philosophy of Right*, pp. 29–30.
[50] *Kritik der praktischen Vernunft, p.* 73 (L. White Beck, p. 64).
[51] *Hegel's Philosophy of Right*, p. 226.

and will along with will and thinking, along with freedom and necessity. The outcome of this change in the notions of Kant and Spinoza is Hegel's evaluation of the social contract.

## 7

Both Spinoza and Kant – in spite of the differences between their respective views – adhered to the concept of social contract. For Spinoza, it is will as desire or appetite which drives men to establish the state, once they have weighed realistically ways and means to preserve their existence. For Kant, the state is established not because of a reciprocal instrumental attitude, but because of the idea of autonomy which amounts to self-legislation. Yet for Kant, too, the fundamental component in the social contract is the component of will, though he cannot avoid the difficulties which arise out of the problematic relationship between will and Reason.

Hegel rejects the idea of social contract:

An association which they enter in relation to some matter is a casual tie arising from the subjective need and choice of the parties. A contract of this kind is essentially distinct from a political bond which is a tie objective, necessary, and independent of choice or whim.[52]

The identical will which is brought into existence by the contract is only one *posited* by the parties, and so is only a will shared in common and not an absolutely universal will.[53]

The social contract is based on, or establishes, the external relation between individuals. An external relation to a common factor is the lowest stage of universality. It was Rousseau's merit to have established the will as the principle of the state.[54] But will is not enough. The grounding of the state in will makes the state a matter of choice or decision. Yet since will and thinking are identical in Hegel, and since both are explications of the Spirit and not acts of decision, the state is an explication – or one of the explications – of Spirit.

Hegel's concern is with "freedom made actual," as he himself puts it in his *Philosophy of Right*.[55] Within the realm of actuality there is no place for the distinction between inner and external, between motive and deed, between the individual as externally related to his fellow

---

[52] "Proceedings of the Estates Assembly in the Kingdom of Württemberg, 1815–1816," in: *Hegel's Political Writings*, tr. T. M. Knox (Oxford 1964) p. 281.

[53] *Hegel's Philosophy of Right*, p. 58.

[54] *Ibid.*, p. 156.

[55] *Ibid.*, p. 20.

individual and to the universal orbit. In Hegel's terms we might say: Spinoza's contract established not a state proper as an actuality of freedom, but only a civil society as a common enterprise directed to the satisfaction of needs, while Kant's – and Fichte's – social contracts do not go beyond the boundaries of the individual will.[56] This is so although will in Kant and Fichte is not "will" in terms of desire as in Spinoza. Yet it is still "will" in terms of the individual person acknowledging the individuality of his fellow man. Conciliation of objective and subjective will cannot be accomplished by Kant, though he aimed at this. This conciliation calls – according to Hegel – for re-evaluation of the relation between the intellectual component and that of will proper.

The supra-individual character of the state cannot be established by a contract. This character must be due to the intellectual component since, as we have seen, it is the aspect of thinking which elevates the particular to the level of universality. This is what leads Hegel to what might be called primacy of speculation over practice in the realm of social life, and, *pari passu*, to the attribution of ethical superiority to the universal over the individual. The social contract was conceived of as being a rational cause of the existence of the state. Hegel does not turn his attention to the cause of existence, but to the substance or meaning of the state, i.e., to the rationality inherent in the actuality. Here again freedom is not a cause, it is a situation.


8

We see clearly that the structure of Hegel's argument *vis-à-vis* substance and subject reemerges *vis-à-vis* necessity and freedom. Correlation of necessity and freedom and their sublation in the totality are a restatement of the same metaphysical situation. The selfsame rhythm prevails in all channels of the discourse, or in all areas of the universe viewed and rendered dialectically.

In terms of the particular position of freedom looked at from a historical perspective, the idea of freedom as inherent in totality emerges as a philosophical view opposed to that represented by Kant, where freedom is a partial causality over against nature, since in Kant nature is represented in the human orbit by man's sensibility. Two positions are formulated here: for Hegel, sensibility is eventually

[56] *S. W.*, XIX, pp. 639.

lifted up to Reason, and thus becomes a part of the totality. Human needs, representing the human earthly situation, are encompassed in the totality of the state or in the totality of the actuality as identical with rationality. Kant's "two trees," i.e. sensibility and Reason, are turned by Hegel into parts of the whole. Human sensibility is not an obstacle in the fulfillment of totality, if there is a continuum from one stage of the human situation to the other.

We have placed Hegel against Kant and Spinoza. It is apposite to consider both Kant and Hegel from the point of view of Marx, in so far as Marx absorbed the two lines of thought – and we shall be returning to Marx at the subsequent stage of this presentation.

Marx follows Hegel to the extent that he does not assume the distinction between sensibility and Reason, or sensibility and freedom. He adheres to the notion of totality. As opposed to Hegel, Marx does not hold that sensibility is to be sublated in Reason and freedom. Reason and freedom are to be realized or actualized on the level of sensibility, that is to say, on the level of human needs as they really are. Kant speaks about pragmatic laws which provide guidance as to how to achieve the goals proposed by our sensible desires. Practical laws proper, whose feature it is to command, do not refer to our sensibility and its aspirations, but are products of pure Reason.[57] Moral laws are for Kant partial laws only, just as pragmatic laws are partial only. The two do not meet in a totality except in the out-of-world sphere, where virtue and satisfaction converge. The notion of totality implies a convergence of human goals and orbits of behavior. It is in this sense that Marx speaks about a theory being realized in a people only to the extent that it is the realization of its needs.[58] The needs which according to Kant belong to the pragmatic sphere, are for Marx the support, the vehicle and the sphere where theory, or the categorical imperative of man as value, is realized.

Systematically and typologically we face here the harmonistic view which is embodied in two theories of totality, and the anti-harmonistic view as it is tied up with the unbridgeable gap between sensibility and Reason. One may wonder whether Kant is right in consigning human needs to the sphere of sensibility, but one may wonder whether Hegel and Marx are right by assuming that all the lines of the universe or

---

[57] B, 828 (632).
[58] *Zur Kritik der Hegelschen Rechtsphilosophie. Einleitung,* in Karl Marx – Friedrich Engels, *Werke* (Berlin 1958), Vol. I, p. 387. The concept of needs (*Bedürfnisse*) was taken over from Hegel's notion of "the system of needs."

of human existence eventually converge, either in speculation or in *praxis*. In any case, the limited concept of freedom, or, to put it differently, looking at freedom as only one line of conduct, has the advantage of being less assuming than the totalistic-harmonistic concept of freedom which eventually brings together necessity and freedom. We emphasize this, viewing that harmony as one of the manifestations of the evolvement of substance into subject.

Before we proceed to the analysis of some further formal aspects of Hegel's system, we should deal with another instance of harmony, that between the universe and philosophy to provide additional facets of the harmony and its structure.

# CHAPTER FIVE

# THE PROCESS AND THE SYSTEM

## I

Our analysis so far leads us to the conclusion that for Hegel there is a twofold beginning which eventually amounts to one, a one endowed with an internal rhythm: the beginning lies in a concept which is "immediate," in the simple relation of the concept to itself. Yet once there is such a relation, the concept cannot rest where it is. It has to move beyond itself to achieve its fulfilment. The beginning is the point of departure endowed with the propensity towards its self-transformation.

This generic theme in Hegel is the theme of transition as a particular and definite interpretation of the rhythm of transformation. The generic process of transformation as fulfilment becomes the concept and orbit of history. History as a process in time is an illustration of the process of fulfilment, as well as one of the manifestations of that process. History is emergent knowledge, that is to say, it has to be viewed as an external manifestation of Spirit in time.[1] This implies that the existence of history depends upon the existence of a spiritual essence which attains self-knowledge by means of the historical process. The self-knowledge of Spirit is not immediately given. To know itself, Spirit – although it is the absolute, real essence – must be unfolded and made externally manifest in a process. Essential to Hegel's explanation of the nature and existence of history is the conception of time as the framework in which Spirit attains externality, and through externality, self-knowledge. This permits him, so to speak, to invoke a self-sustaining, real and absolute essence as ground for history. To put it another way, Hegel's definition of history is at the same time an explanation of its *raison d'être*.

[1] *Phänomenologie* p. 520.

From the definition of history as the external manifestation of Spirit in time, it follows that, were it not for history, Spirit would neither know itself nor prevail in the actual world, that is, in the orbit of becoming. Although it finds reflection in history, the existence of Spirit is not merely historical. Spirit exists as an absolute essence in itself. And it will exist as this essence once its content is made manifest in history and once its self-knowledge is actually adequate to its content. In history, Spirit is diffused, transgressing its internal implicitness to become determined, explicit and articulate in process in time.

In Hegel's approach, history has an auxiliary or functional position of mediation, subservient to Spirit's attainment of self-knowledge. History *qua* occurrence is instrumental – externality in time is for the sake of internality of Spirit. Hegel allots a higher status to the externality of Spirit than to the externality of nature. But the point of Spirit as an expression – alienated one – is that neither manifestation of externality is allotted an independent status, and that both are always presented as subservient to internality. So long as there is mediated becoming for the sake of self-knowledge, history endures, which warrants the assertion that according to Hegel, the existence of history is historical.

Hegel himself says that the concept of Spirit is the foundation of history and that history is the process of Spirit. This process consists in the transcendence by Spirit of its latent self-consciousness for the sake of attaining free self-consciousness. The categorical imperative of Spirit, "Know Thyself," is fulfilled.[2] Plainly, history serves as a field for the fulfilment of a philosophical imperative, the Socratic injunction of self-knowledge. History, then, has a subject – the self-sustaining subject of Spirit. To attain actual self-knowledge, that subject needs time external to itself. Hegel apparently thought that history as an arena of involvement is just another arena like that of the categorial transformation of substance into subject. The duality landing in an identity of potentiality and actuality, with actualization as the middle term between the two, lends itself to application in the orbit of history just as it did to the transition from Reason to Spirit. History is the history of Spirit – this assumption enabled the integration of history into the universal, i.e., not specifically historical, framework of Hegel's conceptual devices.

Hegel "did not take time seriously"; he did not wonder about the

[2] S. W., XIX, pp. 3, 19, 103, 104.

necessary coincidence or identity between conceptual transformation and process in time, a process which is bound to take the shape of the relations which are imposed by the very dimension of time. We are to deal with this central issue in the following Excursus.

The application to time of the universal categorial network amounts, first, to a conceptualization of history and, second, to the view that there is an ultimate stage or an ultimate totality in history. This means that the progressive character of history – and that character is essential since it reflects the rhythm of transformation and achievement – finds its expression in history in certain institutions like the state (to be sure, as interpreted by Hegel), in a certain religion (to be sure, as interpreted by Hegel) and in certain modes of art (again, as interpreted by Hegel) and finally in a certain (in different senses of the term) philosophical system as presented by Hegel as a philosopher living in time. We have already encountered this systematic difficulty in terms of the identity between freedom and necessity – that a line of behaviour sponsored by freedom is viewed as being self-enclosed, lacking both openness toward and serious clash with the necessary conduct of nature or sensibility as an antithesis which cannot be sublated in a synthesis. The harmonization between partial freedom and the total freedom which is absolute necessity, presented serious problems both phenomenologically and systematically. The totalization of occurrences in time and the comprehensive system poses even more serious problems, since thinking human beings exist in time while thinking, among other topics, about time. To "think about" would amount, in Hegel, to the elevation or sublation of the subject-matter of thinking onto the level of the subject of thinking. This indeed is in tune with Hegel's overall trend but one may wonder whether it holds good in the area of history, and not in the area of consciousness only.

The doubts which can be raised regarding Hegel's trend in history can be voiced[3] in even more acute fashion regarding his philosophy of philosophy. This is the topic of our next exploration.

2

In speaking about the nature of philosophy, Kant gave central place to the legislation of human Reason directed toward nature and freedom. The concern of philosophy is with the laws of nature and moral-

---

[3] See the present author's: The Ontological Status of History, *American Philosophical Quarterly*, vol. 9, N. I, January 1972, pp. 49ff.

ity.[4] Laws are concerned with order and regularity, and these formal features, again, apply both to nature and its laws and to morality and its law.

Hegel rejected this view. The laws of phenomena constitute a generalized copy (*Abbild*) of the phenomena themselves.[5] This copy lacks the internal structure of the phenomena, and, being their *Abbild*, it only follows the phenomena. For Hegel, the subject-matter of philosophy is the whole, and he could not, therefore, confine the character of philosophy to the exploration of legislation which applies to data or which is only a form (as in Kantian Ethics) replacing empirical data. Being the cognition of fullness, philosophy is also the self-reflection of the Idea which in turn is identical with being. Here Hegel follows in the footsteps of Aristotle.[6] Once he elaborates the subject-matter of philosophy, Hegel also elaborates what we may call the philosophy of philosophy, that is, the delineation of philosophical thinking as opposed to any other activity of the mind including science, art, religion. Hegel's notion of philosophy as substantive is imbued with his conception of the nature of philosophy, these two aspects of his system being closely interrelated.

In dealing with the nature of philosophical thinking, Hegel attempted a systematic synthesis of two points of view:
(a) philosophy is the self-reflection of the Idea;
(b) philosophy is related to time and to the development of the Idea in time.

In Hegel's opinion these two views are compatible, supplementary and ultimately, identical. The first aspect of his view of the nature of philosophy will be called the "substantive" or "essential" aspect and the second the "epochal" aspect.


3


The difference between Hegel's and Kant's views of the nature of philosophy comes to the fore where Hegel gives to philosophy the task of conceiving that which is,[7] since that which is, is Reason.[8] For Kant philosophy is concerned with Reason, but Reason is not – as we have seen – the totality of the world; concern with Reason can be thus

---

[4] *Kr. d. r. V.*, B 868 (Kemp Smith, p. 658).
[5] *S. W.*, III, p. 105.
[6] *Ibid.*, XVIII, p. 331.
[7] *Hegel's Philosophy of Right*, ed. T. M. Knox, Oxford 1942, p. 11.
[8] *Ibid.*

concern with legislation of data, but not with the overriding whole where Reason would constitute the systematic totality.

Hegel's position implies that philosophical thinking is speculative thinking. It is the object of speculation to conceive all objects, whether of pure thought, of nature or of Spirit, in the form of thought, and thus to conceive of the unity of their differences. In this sense speculation is opposed to reflection, which cannot grasp the unity and which forgets either totality or difference.[9] Reflection here could be taken as Hegel's characterization of Kant's system, although he does not express it this way in the text.

The subject-matter of philosophical cognition is, then, the Idea. Here again Kant differs from Hegel. For Kant, the Idea is a concept composed of notions and exceeding the limits of experience.[10] The Idea is but the extension of the category to the unconditioned – which extension is defined by Kant as speculation.[11] According to Hegel, the conception of the nature of the Idea arises from Kant's initial separation of the legislative aspect of Reason from its actual aspect. For Kant, as Hegel sees him, the highest Idea of philosophy is the total emptiness of subjectivity, the objective practical law being but one of its expressions.[12] For Hegel, the Idea renders the way in which reality is determined by the concept, and as such is the unification of the subjective and the objective.[13]

Philosophy is the cognition of this unification; it is absolute cognition, the concept which entertains itself as object and content and is thus its own actuality.[14] Reason is no longer legislative only. It is substantive or self-reflective in the sense propounded by Aristotle in his concept of *noesis noeseos*. What Aristotle applied to the first mover is applied by Hegel to the whole of reality. Reality is imbued with reflection because reality is the Idea and the Idea cannot but be known. The self-knowledge of the Idea *qua* unity of concept and given data is philosophy. Philosophy as an activity of Reason is by the same token knowledge – and self-knowledge – of the world when there is no separation of Reason from the world. The subject matter of philosophy is the world, and self-knowledge is the subjectivity of the world. The whole world is the self-explication of the *noesis noeseos*. Phi-

---

[9] *S. W.*, XVII, pp. 39–40.
[10] B 377, (Kemp Smith, p. 314).
[11] B 491, B 832. (Kemp Smith p. 422, p. 635).
[12] *S. W.*, I, pp. 326–327.
[13] *S. W.*, III, p. 116.
[14] *Ibid.* p. 84.

losophy has always been concerned with the knowledge of the Idea, and all that merits the name of philosophy takes as basis the consciousness of an absolute unity.[15] The ultimate end and interest of philosophy is the conciliation of thought (the concept) with actuality.[16] Hegel takes advantage here of the term "interest" (*Interesse*) used by Kant, for instance in his three questions,[17] but he does not employ it to describe a mere trend or driving factor of Reason. For Hegel *Interesse* is identical with Reason's goal of its own identity with reality. Kant also uses *Interesse* as a verb, describing the cosmic concept of science as something that necessarily interests (*interessiert*) everybody.[18] Philosophy in the cosmic sense is the science of the relation of all knowledge to the essential ends of human reason (*teleologia rationis humanae*).[19]

In Kant, then, we have the paradoxical situation whereby the *cosmic* aspect of philosophy is related to the objectives of *human* reason, and the interest of human reason is the interest toward these very objectives. In Hegel, Reason is cosmic in the sense that it is related to the world and its interest is directed toward self-realization in and of the world. Kant distinguishes between the "school" meaning of philosophy and its "world" meaning, while for Hegel philosophy is one and cannot be but one. This character of philosophy is based on the oneness of Reason.[20] Here the oneness of philosophy is to be understood as its unity as opposed to the diversity of systems. This program, however, may be applied not only to the history of philosophy but also to Kant's distinctions between the two vistas of philosophy.

4

Philosophy is a world affair since the world as subject matter is *noesis noeseos*. Hence, philosophy as *noesis noeseos* is but the formulation and articulation of the world. The question of finitude and infinity is closely connected with this view. Finitude consists in having a limit; in the limit, the finite something's being is posited, or ceases to be, at the limit, and hence it is related to something else.[21] The

---

[15] *S. W.*, VIII, p. 425.
[16] *S. W.*, XIX, p. 684.
[17] *Kr. d. r. V.*, (Kemp Smith 635).
[18] B 858 (Kemp Smith, p. 651).
[19] *Ibid.*, 866–870.
[20] *S. W.*, I, pp. 185–186.
[21] *Ibid.*, III, p. 42.

philosophical mistake concerning the finite is the assumption of its rigidity, making it into an Absolute, taking it as something permanent whereas it is only finite, thus passing. There is a fundamental contradiction in the realm of the finite in that the finite annuls itself and cannot therefore be taken as persisting.[22] The positing of the finite as an ultimate category involves itself in this contradiction of taking what is passing as ultimate. Hegel plays here with two connotations of finitude: its relation to something outside itself, and its ontological character as passing. Thus, the finite cannot be taken as an independent category since, logically, it calls for a relatum, and ontologically – this distinction has here only a nominal validity – it ceases to be and the question is open what happens with it. Thus, the contradiction cannot be resolved since another relatum is exposed to the same logical and ontological fate as the first.

The structure of *noesis noeseos* defies the structure of finitude. *Noesis noeseos* is self-related, while the finite is other-related. *Noesis noeseos* is a position of arrival, while finite things pass and do not arrive. The denial or negation of finitude is therefore inherent in Hegel's philosophy.

Kant's conception of infinity – the bad or spurious infinity, in Mure's rendering[23] – cannot solve this contradiction. Kant says that the true, i.e., the transcendental concept of infinity is the successive synthesis of unity in measuring a quantum. Successive unity can never be completed. Kant is using here the mathematical concept of infinity which explains given phenomena "as if" the series would be in itself, infinite, i.e., indefinite.[24] Hegel looks at this never-ending process of measuring as caught in the antinomy which the indefinite progress was supposed to solve. The antinomy in Kant leaves both Reason and the phenomena encountered in perception where they were in the first place.[25]

For Kant the Ought (*Sollen*) expresses pure Reason. Reason makes out of its complete spontaneity its own order according to ideas.[26] But clearly this order is one of legislation and not one of self-reflection. The Ought expresses a kind of necessity and connection with Reason which do not occur otherwise in nature.[27] Hence the two orders, of

[22] *Logik*, I, pp. 117ff. (I, pp. 142ff.)
[23] G. R. G. Mure, *A Study of Hegel's Logic* (Oxford 1950), pp. 48ff.
[24] *Kr. d. r. V.*, B 712–713. (Kemp Smith 558–559).
[25] *Logik*, I, pp. 183ff. (204ff.)
[26] *Kr. d. r. V.*, B 576 (473).
[27] *Ibid.*, B 575 (Kemp Smith p. 472).

nature and of the Ought, do not meet, and provide neither for totality nor for the subject matter of philosophy as totality.

Philosophy, for Hegel, is not merely a powerless Idea which remains an unrealizable Ought;[28] it is concerned with full reality and the realization of all potentialities. As the Aristotelian first cause is pure *energeia* with no ingredient of potentiality to be found in it, so actuality or being in its fullness contains the ethical imperative, Kant's Ought. The realized Ought ceases to be an Ought only, and becomes immersed in actuality.

Philosophy as concerned with being as identical with thought, or philosophy as the expression of *noesis noeseos* cannot assume that pure Reason expresses itself in an independent order different from that of nature. It expresses itself in the comprehensive order of reality. True infinity is reflection in itself.[29] It is not a relation of dependence on something outside, but is the self-contained character of reality. Hence the subject-matter of philosophy is true infinity as *noesis noeseos* and philosophy is itself that *noesis noeseos*. Infinity is not an extension of the finite. It is the other way around – the finite is the appearance of infinity. Here the religious world view which looks at the world as at a manifestation of God (theophany) served Hegel as his model.[30] For Kant eternity meant the end of all things; he addressed himself to eternity in the moral context and spoke about its awe-inspiring majesty.[31] For Hegel the true annulment of time is the timeless present. Here the strife, strivings and absolute oppositions are removed.[32] We emphasize striving, because the elimination of striving brings Hegel's concept of eternity close to that of Aristotle, who also combined eternity with actuality.[33] The absence of striving places eternity, as a self-contained entity, beyond the moral struggle and progress emphasized by Kant. Eternity was not, and will not be; it is.[34] Hegel's interpretation of eternity differs from that of Spinoza for whom existence necessarily follows from the definition of eternal. Hegel relates eternity to the present, thus pointing to a dimension in time which supposedly has no meaning in terms of time. This is a dilemma of the Hegelian system related to what we have called the

---

[28] *Encykl.* § 6.
[29] *S. W.*, III p. 131.
[30] *S. W.*, XV, pp. 209–210.
[31] *Kritik der praktischen Vernunft*, ed. by K. Vorländer (Leipzig, 1929), p. 168. (Lewis Beck's trans. p. 152).
[32] *S. W.*, I, p. 97.
[33] *Metaphysics* 1071b.
[34] *Encykl.* § 259.

"epochal" aspect in his program of philosophy. Hegel tries to formulate an "is" (*ist*) which does not have a temporal meaning, yet in finding some affinity between *ist* and *jetzt* he involves himself in problems which are perhaps insoluble.

We have now to consider Hegel's conception of time. Such an analysis is essential insofar as we are concerned with the relation between philosophy as having a definite subject-matter, and its changing aspects including philosophical systems occurring in time.

5

It is said, Hegel notes, that everything comes to be and ceases to be in time. More correct would be to say that time itself is this coming to be, becoming and vanishing.[35] This comment is directed against the view that time is an abstract form disconnected from that which occurs in it, time being either measure of motion or an empty framework within which occurrences take place successively. Being the process itself, time is the existence of this perpetual self-annulment and self-sublation (*sich-Aufheben*).[36] Ceasing to exist is a negation. Time as this perpetual ceasing to be, annuls that which was. It is the negation of the negation, or, the negation related to itself.

Does this last statement express what Hegel really attempted to convey? The negation of the negation is a perpetual linear process. Where does the self-relation take place? Hegel did not deny the irreversibility of time and succession. Since there is an order according to which "b" follows "a," how could he speak of times as self-referential "*die sich auf sich beziehende Negation*"?[37] If Hegel meant that "b" negates "a" and "c" negates "b," etc., then this would be negation *in* time but not negation *of* time. Hegel should have distinguished between formal time and that which takes place in time, but instead he tried to get rid of this distinction. Hence, time is the being which through *that* which it is – is not, and through that which it is not, is.[38]

Thus time is not identical with the fullness of being, which is identical with Reason. Time cannot be a part of the *noesis noeseos*, as it was not in Aristotle. Hegel faced a difficulty here, or what might seem to be a difficulty, because he included the world within the *noesis noeseos*,

35 *Encykl.* § 258.
36 *Ibid.*, § 257, Zusatz.
37 *Ibid.*
38 *Ibid.*, § 258.

not confining the latter structure to the extra-mundane first mover as did Aristotle. How can the world be a *noesis noeseos* and still have the time dimension? Hegel had to face this problem; the question is whether he really solved it or left it without a solution, or remained within his own ambivalence on this issue.

A distinction has to be made between time and the Idea as subject matter of philosophy, or the world conceived of philosophically. As against the becoming and ceasing to be of time, the true or the Idea or the Spirit are eternal.[39] Eternity connotes here a level of being above time which cannot find its manifestation in the structure and rhythm of time.[40] The fact that actual things are incongruous with the Idea is the finite element in them, the element of lack of truth.[41] If time is coming to be and ceasing to be, it is related to finitude. Finitude is not a component of the Idea. Thus the Idea is incongruous with time. The Idea as the unity of the concept with objectivity is a situation, a self-referential and self-reflective situation. It cannot be related to time, in spite of the hint at self-relation in time which we discussed above. The Idea is the end and not the process.

One cannot help discerning Hegel's fascination with time. According to the conception of philosophy by which its definite subject-matter is found in the identity of Reason and actuality – no dimension of time can be applied to the subject-matter of philosophy, nor can time have part in the characterization of its nature. Yet Hegel does use an aspect of time in order to bring forward the nature of philosophy. Philosophy is not lost in the past, since the Idea is present (*präsent*). The Spirit is immortal, that is to say, it does not pass and is not nothing, it is essentially *itzt* (archaic form of the German *jetzt*).[42] We may conjecture from this text that Hegel is looking for a *tertium comparationis* between eternity in his own sense and time, or the dimension of time which is the proper one for this undertaking, i.e., present time. The present connotes both that which is there *in* the present as well as the *locus* of being there. For Hegel, who does not allow for time as a mere form, these two aspects of the present cannot be separated. Hegel gives clear preference to the present over the other dimensions of time: only the present is, the before and after are not; but the

---

[39] *Ibid.*
[40] *S. W.*, XII, p. 454.
[41] *Logik*, II, p. 440 (II, p. 426).
[42] *S. W.*, XI, p. 120.

concrete present is the result of the past and is inseminated by the future. Therefore, the truth present is eternity.[43]

We should be cautious at this point, since Hegel uses the expression *"true present,"* possibly suggesting a distinction between present in the plain sense of the term and a *true* present. We may, however, discern an analogy between present as the dimension of time and eternity as being here, with the *tertium comparationis* between eternity and present being the presence of the content. Eternity would be an amplification of the present and the present would be an illustration or contraction of eternity. One could say that the notion of *analogia entis* is implied here, or that Hegel looks at the present from what might be called the *eucharistic* point of view: the Lord is present in his bodily expression, his presence is real and still only symbolic or manifested. The present for Hegel is in a way a kind of fullness, though not a constant one. Still, since the present absorbs the past and carries within itself the seeds of the future it is indeed a fullness, though a "pointillistic" one.

The present was for Hegel a position inherently related to the past and to the future, negating the past and bearing it, negating the future and pointing to it, making it emerge. The relational structure of time viewed from its position of the present was for Hegel an additional factor in his fascination with time. We notice the difference between Hegel, Plato and Kant in their respective evaluations of time. For Plato, time is the moving likeness of eternity, and it seems to be correct to underline the word *moving*. For Plato, Heaven is a thing that has been and is and shall be perpetually. Perdurance throughout time is the illustration of eternity. Eternity is not understood as perpetuality in time; perpetuality is patterned on eternity. Hegel looked at the present not as a moving likeness of eternity, but, on the contrary, as a standing-still likeness of eternity. Fullness in time and not the extension of time provides for the analogy between eternity and time.

If we look at time in Kant's system, we notice that his emphasis is on time as a series in which the order of synthesis is determined. It is not the present, but succession as such which is the focal point and the essential characteristic of Kant's view of time. Since there is a given order in time, time can be the point of departure and the *locus* of realization of an order established in and through the categorial apparatus. Again, since the center of gravitation of Kant's system is the

---

[43] *Encykl.* § 259, Zusatz.

legislative aspect of Reason, Kant looks for an aspect of time where this legislative capacity and function can be realized. He finds the primordial order of time congenial to the superstructure of a conceptual order imposed on that time-order.[44] For Hegel, the central issue is fullness. He discerns the ingredient of fullness in time, and does not attribute a central position to order in time. For Hegel, the position of now (*jetzt*) is an illustration of the dialectic of transition from one to another; it is both another and one and the same, because of the relation between past and future at both ends, and the now of the present[45] in the middle.

An additional comparison is called for at this juncture. Whitehead says:

The World which emphasizes the multiplicity of moral things is the World of Activity. It is the World of Origination: It is the Creative World. It creates the Present by transforming the Past, and by anticipating the Future. When we emphasize sheer Active Creation, the emphasis is upon the Present – namely, upon "Creative Now," where the reference to transition has been omitted ... "Creative Now" is a matter-of-fact which is one aspect of the Universe – namely, the fact of immediate origination. The notions of Past and Future are then ghosts within the fact of the Present.[46]

The essential aspect of the present is, for Whitehead, *origination*; for Hegel, the central point is the *presence* of a content. For Whitehead, the central point is the transformation of the past through the creative present; for Hegel it is the accumulation of the past in the process of transmission and the fading away of the past. Accumulation is most prominent in Hegel's approach to the history of philosophy.

7

We have referred to the epochal component in Hegel's philosophy. *Epoche* denotes a holding point. Hence, there is even a connection between *epoche* as a holding point in time and *epoche* as witholding judgment as advocated by the skeptics. The epochal component in Hegel is related to time. Yet time is not only a series of disconnected nows. Moreover, in spite of the prominence of the "now," it is meaningless unless it is positioned against the past and the future. This is

---

[44] Consult the present author's *Experience and its Systematization*, Studies in Kant (The Hague 1965) pp. 31ff. Second edition 1972.

[45] *S. W.*, XVIII, 383–384.

[46] See A. N. Whitehead, "Immortality," in: *Essays in Science and Philosophy* (New York 1948), pp. 61–62.

the case with regard to time in general; it is even more so with regard
to history as a series of *Geschehnisse*. Indeed, speaking about history
Hegel speaks about a heritage and the result of labour, i.e., the labour
of the preceding generation of humankind.[47] Continuity is implied in
the concept of heritage-continuity in time.

Hegel (we deliberately confine ourselves here to philosophy and its
history without going into the question of history at large – some extension of this will be found in the following Excursus) is again caught
in a dilemma: he has to assume that philosophy is always concerned
with the same subject-matter. Yet in so far as he refers to time he is
bound at this juncture to "take time seriously" defying his self-
consistence: time in general, various periods of time, and his own time
in particular. Regarding the constant subject-matter he says that the
history of philosophy exhibits through the various philosophies only
one single philosophy (*eine Philosophie*). The various philosophies are
related to particular principles, but these particular and partial
principles are only branches of one and the same whole.[48] This would
amount to the presence of philosophy in all times and in every single
segment of time. Yet Hegel also maintained the view that the latest,
most recent philosophy, is the most developed, the richest and the
deepest.[49] This would mean that there is development in philosophy
by which the period more advanced in the time succession coincides
with the content more adequate *vis-à-vis* the program of philosophy.
Again, this view on the congruence between time and content clashes
with the view that the history of philosophy is concerned with that
which never ages, with that which is presently (again: *gegenwärtig*)
alive.[50]

The dialectical development of the subject-matter of philosophy as
*noesis noeseos* breaks through the ever-ceasing character of time.
Philosophy preserves its character in spite of the changing times and
finds its adequate manifestations historically, within time. *Noesis
noeseos* is there, and does not develop; how can it be conceived as
placed in time? Hegel seems to suggest that *noesis* is not only the
reflection of *noetos qua* being in its identity with Reason, but that
there is also a *noesis* on the part of the finite human beings who
entertain the *noetos* in time and who ultimately express it adequately.

---

[47] *S. W.*, XVII, pp. 28–29.
[48] *Ibid.*, VI, p. 25.
[49] *Ibid.*, XVII, p. 71.
[50] *Ibid.*, p. 69.

There is *noesis* within the self-contained *noesis noeseos* and there is an open *noesis* carried out and carried by human subjects. Hegel is bound to assume a pre-established harmony between the *noesis* of the finite human beings emerging in time and vanishing in it in accordance with the structure and the rhythm of time, and the *noesis* which is eternally and *ab initio* engaged in the *noesis noeseos*. Without a pre-established harmony, refuge can be sought only in lucky accident, which is but a resigned version of pre-established harmony. Diffusiveness in time and the intensity of eternity are different structures. The harmony between the two is a *tour de force* of the system, but at the same time it is a manifestation of force.[51]

Concerning the Spirit of the World, Hegel says that it has enough time, and that it invests a tremendous lavishness in becoming and vanishing. The way of the Spirit is mediation, the way about or detour (*Umweg*).[52] Yet, that the Spirit of the World has enough time implies the prior assumption that it has time at all; that it moves through a *detour* implies that it has a *tour*. Now, these assumptions do not follow from the inner structure of Spirit. They are impositions on the Spirit or on the world as *noesis noeseos*, to absorb time into the structure, or to exhibit the structure in time. These assumptions are the consequence of an attempt to make finite consciousness, not a correlate of the world, but an appearance of the world or an emanation of it. Yet this is a strange emanation indeed: the human finite consciousness is not only at a less complete level, but in its incompleteness it retains its capacity to grasp the *noesis noeseos* as it stands prior to emanation, still and independent of the detour of human consciousness.

After all, it is human consciousness which, by its immanent dialectic, grasps the identity of Reason and being. This consciousness does not call for an act of redemption to come from an external agent in order to lift it up to the adequate conception of the identity of Reason and being. Either *noesis noeseos* does not need time at all, and then enough time is of no consequence, or else even enough time will not resolve the dilemma and bring about the identification of the human *noesis* with the *noesis noeseos*. The essential component in Hegel's philosophy does not need the assistance of the epochal component; the epochal cannot elevate itself to the level of the essential.

There is here a fundamental difference between Aristotle and Hegel:

---

[51] This interpretation differs from that of Alexandre Kojève, who identifies eternity and time in Hegel. Consult his *Introduction à la lecture de Hegel* (Paris 1947), pp. 336ff.
[52] *S. W.*, XVII, pp. 65–66.

*noesis noeseos*, in Aristotle, as the subject matter of metaphysics is the object of theoretical thinking. It points to the ultimate fulfillment of theory but does not make theory on the human level into *noesis noeseos*. Thus there is a distinction between understanding an object and understanding itself. For Hegel this distinction disappears. Aristotle philosophizes from the position of a finite intellect. Hegel believes that in philosophizing the finite intellect ceases to be finite. Philosophy is not an activity only. It is the end – the ultimate and the objective end. The difference between Hegel and Aristotle here is due to the different positions of the *noesis noeseos*: for Aristotle it is the essence of the detached unmoved mover. For Hegel it is spread over the cosmos and embraces in itself the finite human intellect.[53]

## 8

The congruence between finite intellect and infinite knowledge of the infinite is implied in Hegel's notion of the relationship between philosophy and time, time as *Zeitalter*, i.e., a period of time or a segment of time. Time in this sense has a topological meaning denoting a "now" (*jetzt*), not merely a "now" experienced by an individual within the orbit of his particular encounter with the world. It is, as it were, a prolonged "now," an extended "now" of many individuals which takes the shape of a period in time to be defined not chronologically, or only chronologically, as, e.g., 1789–1831, but in terms of an overriding unity which bestows on the period its distinctive features as the era of enlightenment, romanticism, constitutional monarchy, and the like.

The relation of philosophy to its time is one of determination by that period of time: "It is absurd to fancy that a philosophy can transcend its contemporary world ..."[54] Yet we have to look closely at Hegel's argument for this determining capacity of the period of time: "To comprehend what is, is the task of philosophy, because what is, is Reason."[55] Time's determination of philosophy is ultimately the determination by Reason of philosophy as an activity of Reason. Reason is in the first place the conception of that which is; it is related to eternity as that which is. The "now" in time serves, as we have seen before, as a

---

[53] On the relevance of this to the feature of finitude in human nature see the present author's: *Spirit and Man*, The Hague 1963, pp. 112ff.
[54] Hegel's *Philosophy of Right*, p. 11.
[55] *Ibid.*

hint toward the direction of the eternal presence. We see that Hegel takes this structure of the relationship between Reason and being and transplants it into the relationship between a partial being (that aspect of what there is as it is found embodied ln the contemporary world) and the partial philosophical system which is determined by that partial being. This determination by being states not only the positive content that a particular philosophy can have, but also sets the limit to what a particular philosophy can attempt to be. It cannot attempt to transcend determination on the part of its period.

One has to ask wherefrom does Hegel draw the conclusion that there is no spontaneity on the level of philosophy which can carry it beyond the enclosure of the segment of reality in time. If the segment is Reason, why it is a confined, limited Reason? Suppose it is limited because it fills a limited span of time: why should Reason on the level of philosophy be limited too, or why should it lack the spontaneity to go beyond the determining Spirit of its time? Hegel seems to have held this view because he suspected that to allow a partial philosophical system the capacity to transcend reality would mean allowing it to transcend being in general, and to do this would destroy the possibility of identifying Reason and being. The program of Hegel's philosophy, or of philosophy as Hegel viewed it[56] would be essentially undermined. Now, this seems to be faulty reasoning, if indeed this reasoning underlies Hegel's presentation of his argument. What we encounter here is an *analogia entis* in reverse: just as the structure of infinite reasoning was bestowed on the structure of finite reasoning, so here the limitation of finite reasoning, which forbids its transcending a given climate of opinion or Spirit of time, is imposed on infinite reasoning which is also forbidden to transcend. Yet there is nothing to be transcended in *noesis noeseos*. To transcend a given fragment of reality might be a feature of a finite intellect, while to remain within the relationship of identity with reality as a totality would remain the very definition of infinite intellect. Hence there is nothing wrong in the philosophical position that finitude *ought* to be annulled,[57] since an ought is an expression of a semi-independent intellect, a finite intellect whose finitude need not condemn it to be determined only by that which already is. A piecemeal transformation of that which is, is possibly a less spectacular performance for a finite intellect than its elevation to a grasp of

---

[56] On Hegel's program of philosophy see W. Marx, *Die Bestimmung der Philosophie im deutschen Idealismus* (Stuttgart 1964).

[57] *Encykl.* § 36.

infinity.[58] But this transformation is an expression of the spontaneous intellect just the same. Hegel clings here to the principle: everything or nothing.

Particular philosophies are not vogue philosophies. Hegel says: "They are not fortuitous, just lightning, straw-fire."[59] Yet it seems that he sets up the dichotomy with exaggerated sharpness: the philosophies are not vogue philosophies but *Philosophy*, the disclosing of God as he knows himself.[60] Hegel seems to be looking for an anchor for philosophy, and the anchor he finds is twofold – reality in its partiality, and God who knows himself. These two anchors are eventually one, since it is through these partial realities that God knows himself. An independent finite intellect seemed powerless to Hegel; he did not acknowledge the semi-capacity of a semi-dependent and semi-independent intellect. If philosophy is determined by a segment of reality and if it is but time conceived in concepts, then reality seems to be the potentiality of philosophy and philosophy the actuality of reality. It is questionable whether this rhythm of potentiality and actuality suits the relationship between reality and the intellect.

The consequence of the distinction between the essential and the epochal – epochal being in this case the contemporary Spirit – is expressed in the statement that the particular interest of our time is to conceive the relation between the concept and being. The greatness of the contemporary world lies in the subject's deepening within himself, in the finite's knowing himself as infinite.[61] Thus Hegel's own philosophy is the adequate expression and manifestation of his time. This leads unavoidably to the circular argument which characterizes this reasoning: the manifest philosophy determines the trend of the *Zeitgeist*, while the *Zeitgeist* is supposed to find its expression in the manifest philosophy. Applying here the difference and the relation between potentiality and actuality, we can say that from the point of view of things, philosophy determines the features of the *Zeitgeist*, while from the point of view of precedence in time, the *Zeitgeist* determines the character of philosophy. This circular relationship draws philosophy into a difficult and problematic situation. In order to avoid its stigmatization as mere vogue-philosophy, Hegel feels compelled to consider one particular philosophical system as the

---

[58] *S. W.*, XV, p. 334.
[59] *Ibid.*, XIX, p. 686.
[60] *Ibid.*
[61] *S. W.*, XVI, pp. 211–212.

legitimate and adequate manifestation of the latent and inarticulate *Zeitgeist*.

One may ask whether both Kant and Hegel belong to the same contemporary world, or whether one should observe the calendar-succession and look at Hegel as belonging to a time – and *a fortiori* to the Spirit of a time – different from that of Kant.[62] Empirically, in terms of the text and of the interwovenness of the problems and of their solutions, a strict correspondence whereby succession in time means elevation and enhancement of the substance of the respective philosophical systems, does not seem warranted.

Ultimately, Hegel goes beyond the model of incarnation and a eucharistic expression. For him the finite leads harmoniously to the infinite and the infinite exhibits itself exhaustively in the finite: "The upward and the downward path are one."

What emerges from the preceding analysis can be summed up as follows: The subject matter of philosophy is the totality of the world. Yet the world is not a static unit; it evolves in time and is engaged in the exhibition of its intrinsic qualities. This again is one of the meanings of the shift from substance to subject. The evolvement of the world is *Verwirklichung*, fulfillment, realization. The meaning of realization in this context is action or activity bringing about a result, though this result is only the manifestation of the latent content.

Yet there is a peculiar relationship between the world as a subject-matter and philosophy as reflection on the world. The other meaning of the world "realization" brings that peculiarity into prominence: realization is making real as an object of thought. It is a process or procedure of bringing an object or a content before one's mind. Philosophy is the realization of the world in the two senses: in philosophy the world gets to be known, and as known it is fulfilled. To be at the end and to be known are eventually identical. There is a cosmic significance to philosophy just as there is a reflective aspect to the world.

9

Let us restate some of the dilemmas Hegel is bound to face on account of his twofold evaluation of philosophical systems: on the one hand,

---

[62] The historical present has, clearly, a bearing on the structure of historical time in general. In spite of his overwhelming concern with history, Hegel is not particularly helpful on this issue. See the present author's *Between Past and Present. An Essay on History* (New Haven 1958), pp. 51ff.

looking at philosophy as bound to the Spirit of the times, on the other seeing a progressive character in the movement from one era to the next, which movement is thus a movement from one articulation of the Spirit in time to another more advanced articulation of the Spirit of the subsequent time.

Hegel has a definite predilection for Greek philosophy – one has only to be reminded of his admiration for Parmenides on the one hand and for Heraclitus on the other. Yet he has to provide room for the subsequent development of philosophy even though he is not unaware of the fundamental difference of mere stature between, let us say, Medieval philosophy and Ancient philosophy. How can he resolve, or try to resolve, this clash between his estimation of Greek philosophy and his recognition, not only of the legitimacy of subsequent periods but even the superiority of these periods, since he is guided by the principle that the subsequent is essentially superior to the preceding periods and the articulations which they achieved?

The clue to the resolution of the dilemma seems to lie in two related assumptions. The first is that the recognition of substance precedes the evolvement of subject, or, in other words, that the awareness that philosophy is concerned with the totality of the world precedes, theoretically as well as historically, the conceptual articulation and determination of that totality. Hence both theoretically, phenomenologically and historically – let us say chronologically – the principle of Greek philosophy has to precede the principle of the Christian philosophy of the Middle Ages as well as the philosophy of the modern era. After all, Hegel himself says[63] that the principle of Christianity is the truth of the idea of Spirit as concrete Spirit. Man ought to know himself in God. Thus, Christianity, and philosophy expressing the *Zeitgeist* of Christianity, articulate an essential philosophical concept – that of concrete Spirit. In both Christian and philosophical terminology they articulate the principle of reconciliation as the unity of the finite subject with the infinite.[64] The greatness of the classical philosophical system is, as it were, supplemented by the discovery of reconciliation, thus adumbrating that which has to be the ultimate philosophical synthesis.

Yet the discovery of Spirit in subjectivity leads to a dialectical development which seems to sever the ties between subjectivity and substance. Once the stress is laid on consciousness, it is not enough to

[63] S. W., XIX, pp. 108–110.
[64] *Idem*, pp. 102–103.

declare the unity between consciousness and being. Consciousness itself undergoes a process of articulation. This is a progressive step since it brings into prominence the richness of the categorial structure of subjectivity, but at the same time it separates the articulated subjectivity from being and substance. Indeed, this is what Hegel claims is a principal feature of Kant's philosophy. The content of that philosophy, he says, is not knowledge of the Absolute but knowledge of subjectivity.[65] Or else, strongly worded: "the speculative idea deprived of its power (*depotenzierte spekulative Idee*)."[66] Hegel characterizes this tendency of Kant's thinking thus: our thinking, our spiritual activity, is conceived as the evil. Hegel comments that we encounter here an enormous humility (*Demut*) of the Spirit, not to rely on knowing.[67] This amounts to the conclusion that Reason cannot give reality to ideas, or that being cannot be picked out of a concept.[68]

A price is paid for the emergence of subjectivity; the Spirit of the world has to pay a price for the achievement of self-awareness. The price is that the overemphasized subjectivity is powerless with regard to actuality. It might be apposite to call Hegel's view of the entire philosophical development a kind of philosophical theodicy. In his attempt to vindicate what has been achieved, he gives to his theodicy a completely intellectual character. Unlike traditional theodicies which attempt to justify *evil* deeds, Hegel attempts to justify *errors*. He says this explicitly: theodicy, a justification of God, is a correction of our idea, pointing out that the world is going its way in a reasonable manner (*vernünftig in der Welt zugegangen*).[69]

10

The fact that Hegel takes such strong exception to his contemporaries who themselves criticize excessive subjectivity, is only a confirmation of what we are after here. To jump over subjectivity without retaining the categorial articulation which a philosophy of consciousness and subjectivity brought about, points to the direction of the real philosophical synthesis but it does not bring about that synthesis. The bone of contention here is of course the concept of intellectual intuition – and the philosophical position represented by Schelling in which that

[65] S. W., I, p. 296.
[66] S. W., III, pp. 310–311.
[67] S. W., XVII, p. 343.
[68] S. W., III, pp. 310–311.
[69] Idem, p. 104.

intuition is central. Intellectual intuition is an immediate consciousness of the identity between subject and object, but as such it lacks categorial determination. Even more so, being an intuition (*Anschauung*), it remains a subjective postulate[70] in spite of the fact that it pretends to overcome subjectivity. Schelling does not move further than Spinoza. In Spinoza's definitions the highest speculative component has been laid down, but only in the form of assurances. The same applies to Schelling.[71] Thus the progress, if any, from mere subjectivity to the Absolute via intellectual intuition is in the re-discovery of the horizon of the Absolute, but not in the establishment of a dialectical synthesis between subject and being, or in the elevation of substance to subject.

This view of the progress of the history of philosophy, with all the innuendoes of its theodicy, is echoed in one of the most problematic aspects of Hegel's philosophy of philosophy or his own self-evaluation. Every philosophical system, being an articulation of the Spirit of the time, is finite by the very position of the Spirit of the time. Conceptually, a philosophical system emphasizing substance is finite, since it emphasizes only one pole of the ultimate synthesis. The same applies to philosophical systems emphasizing the pole of subjectivity, or even to those systems emphasizing the reconciliation between the two poles, but a reconversion lacking dialectical exposition. This view is of course related to Hegel's version of what he calls "Idealism": the proposition that the finite is ideal (*ideell*) constitutes Idealism. Idealism in philosophy consists of nothing else than not recognizing the finite as veritable being.[72] The Introduction to the *Philosophy of Right* expresses it even more strongly:

Philosophy has to do with Ideas, and therefore not with what are commonly dubbed mere concepts. On the contrary, it exposes such concepts as one-sided and false, while showing at the same time that it is the concept alone (not the mere abstract category of the understanding which we often hear called by the name) which has actuality, and further that it gives this actuality itself. All else, apart from this actuality, established through the working of the concept itself, is ephemeral existence, external contingency, opinion, unsubstantial appearance, falsity, illusion and so forth. The shapes which the concept assumes in the course of its actualization are indispensable for the knowledge of the concept itself.[73]

---

[70] *S. W.*, XIX, p. 655.
[71] *Encykl.* § 229, Zusatz.
[72] *Logik*, I, p. 145 (I, p. 168; the translation has been amended here.)
[73] *Hegel's Philosophy of Right*, translated with Notes by T. M. Knox, Oxford 1942, p. 14.

We cannot avoid noting Hegel's ambivalence when reading this text. On the one hand, mere concepts are unsubstantial appearance. On the other hand, every finite manifestation, including mere concepts, is an indispensable shape which the concept assumes for its knowledge of itself. In so far as Hegel's theodicy rejects the finite it integrates the finite into the infinite system. Not only is the world infinite but the system is infinite, too. In his eager drive to achieve ultimate synthesis, Hegel did not notice the preponderance of the world as the subject matter of philosophy, and attempted to transplant the infinity of the world onto the philosophical system referring to the world. He did not want to recognize that articulation of the world can never reach the level of infinity, since the shapes of the world vary in historical and intellectual circumstances, thus calling upon a philosophical system not only to integrate the world but to integrate experience of the world. It is not so that a philosophical system approaches a world constantly given; it approaches the world taking into account the open-ended character of human experience. The world viewed as a closed universe is experienced differently than the world viewed as an open universe. And an open universe in the space-age is experienced differently than the open universe as experienced by Pascal. This is one formulation of a principal issue involved: philosophy is not just a conceptual articulation of substance but also a conceptual interpretation of human encounters, and these, even when we assume that they have a cumulative character, do not necessarily have a progressive character,[74] let alone a character of an ultimate consummation to be achieved in a philosophical system, be it a very great philosophical system.

Even when we assume that there is a cosmic significance to philosophy, philosophy is not the cosmos, and the cosmos is not philosophy. Hegel is propounding the notion that philosophy is the realization of the world, but this notion becomes a stumbling block to the development of some of the basic concepts of Hegel's system. We will presently be concerned with dialectic as realization, and further, with the ambiguity of dialectical realization.

---

[74] On the problem of progress see the present author's "The Idea of Historical Progress and its Assumptions" in: *History and Theory* Vol. X, 2, 1971, pp. 197ff. On the impossibility of an ultimate philosophy consult the present author's book: *Philosophy – The Concept and its Manifestations*, Dordrecht 1972, pp. 176ff.

# CHAPTER SIX

# THE FIRST AND THE SECOND SYNTHESIS

## I

The term "dialectic" has already appeared at several points in our discussion. We will now look into the essence of dialectic as such. It is mandatory to explore the formal structure of the dialectical shifts as they emerge at different junctures of Hegel's system.

It is advisable to preface this exploration by a few comments on dialectic in general. The term "dialectic," like some other philosophical terms, has penetrated into the everyday vocabulary of the last generations. Because the term now has its own impact and field of associations, it is apposite to look into the "hard" concept of dialectic present in Hegel in comparison with what might be viewed as a kind of "soft" version of dialectic.

Goethe spoke about the cultivation of the spirit of contradiction, that spirit which was given to man in order to enable him to learn to recognize the difference of things. We take up from this *bon mot* the emphasis on recognition of difference, and apply it to the first variety of the "soft" dialectic. Our first example will be from De Saussure's theory of language:

> ... in language there are only differences. Even more important: a difference generally implies positive terms between which the difference is set up; but in language there are only differences *without positive terms*. A linguistic system is a series of differences of sound, combined with a series of differences of ideas ... the pairing of a certain number of acoustical signs.[1]

The difference of mere opposition referred to is the difference e.g., between l and r, or that in the group of labials between p and b, or in

---

[1] Ferdinand De Saussure, *Course in General Linguistic*, ed. Bally – A. Sechehaye in collaboration with A. Reidlinger, tr. Wade Baskin (New York 1950), p. 120.

the group of dentals between t and d, etc.[2] To be sure, De Saussure's argument does not point to the transition from one phoneme to another, that is to say, p does not get transformed into b, nor does it find its supplement in b. Opposition as such is present. To express it in Hegel's terms, the differences, even when presented as oppositions, are not resolved in a totality comprising p and b. Insofar as language is understood as a sum total of phonemes, there is no possible meaning to a totality harmonizing the phonemes, since such a totality would do away with the character of language. De Saussure speaks about "the sign in its totality," intending to underline that "only if the signified and the signifier are considered separately" is it true that everything in language is negative; "when we consider the sign in its totality, we have something that is positive in its own class."[3] The shift from the negative to the positive, if it is a shift at all, amounts to seeing the positive as the other side of the negative. No new meaning comes to the fore.

De Saussure's presentation, closely tied up with the notion of difference as such, may – not, however without a certain shift – lead to a dialectical interpretation. Claude Levi-Strauss gives this dialectical interpretation to language: "Linguistics ... presents us with a dialectical and totalizing entity ..."[4] One may grant the correctness of relating dialectic to totalization, yet one may doubt whether the nature of language permits this dialectic interpretation. Levi-Straus is inclined to see oppositions as dialectical pairs, but one may wonder whether the opposition of raw and cooking, boiling and roasting, and other "binary" oppositions are, as a matter of fact, dialectical oppositions. Even when we grant that these oppositions exhaust the totality, e.g., ways of cooking, we cannot assume that one way of cooking leads to another as substance leads to subject or Reason to Spirit. We have seen the stumbling block of dialectic in the Hegelian sense in the supposed transition from Spirit to history. *A fortiori* this is the case with a list of differences presented as if it were comprised in a dialectical movement and conception, viz., whether or not we retain the differences or else lift them up to a harmonizing totality.

Yet, insofar as we do not insist on a strict understanding of dialectic in its fundamental structure, and allow for a "softer" version of it, we may adjust ourselves to the position that there are cases of blurring

[2] *Ibid.*, p. 45.
[3] *Ibid.*, p. 120.
[4] Claude Levi-Straus, *The Savage Mind* (La Pensée sauvage) (London 1962), p. 252.

of distinctions between differences as such, and differences looked at dialectically. The crucial point is in the question of the nature of the synthesis and totality and in their position in the system.[5]

2

The differences between the phonemes are ultimate facts. Hence it is senseless to suppose that there can be sublation of their differences. Phonemes are different; but they are not one-sided. Another version of dialectic, somewhere between the "soft" and the "hard" species, is the dialectic or quasi-dialectic related to the overcoming of one-sided-ness.

Let us take an example from the social sphere, since in that sphere dialectic is so often applied, and one may wonder what sort of dialectic it is. Take the instance of market economy based on competition between individuals and groups. It is the task and fate of each individual, out of his own initiative and adjustment to the situation, to find his place in the economy and to safeguard his share in the sum total of available commodities and services. A dialectical view proper is that which argues, as Marx did, that the market economy itself carries with itself its own dissolution, that is to say, creates its own defeat. The clash between the market economy and its antithesis brings about a new economy which will eventually create the situation: from each according to his ability, for each according to his needs. We do not question here whether this dialectical model is warranted by historical events. We point only to the model itself.

But take a different approach: the modern welfare state is not based on the concept of the self-transformation of the market economy and its ultimate resolution in a new economic structure. It is based on the notion of mitigation of the problems and sharp edges created by the market economy by way of providing – free – services in health, education, unemployment relief, care for the aged, etc. Thus, individuals are involved in the market economy and share its fate, but not all the areas of their lives are exposed to its consequences. Together

---

[5] The linguistic analysis of oppositions sounds like a reverse statement of Spinoza's *Omnis determinatio est negatio*. But this is not so: Spinoza's proposition intends to emphasize that any particular determination of substance imposes limitations on substance and thus undermines its inherent infinity, whereas the linguistic analysis starts off with particular sounds and eventually is left with particular sounds. This again is related to the problem of totality as Hegel saw it, when he pointed out that in Spinoza's view there is only one substance. This follows from the relationship between Spinoza's senses of determination and negation. See *Logik*, I, p. 100, (I, 125).

with their involvement in the market system, they rely on checks and balances against that system. Here there is an implicit or explicit acknowledgement of the one-sidedness of the market economy in meeting human needs and expectations; there is no reliance on the self-regulating character of the market economy to overcome out of its own resources its own crises and catastrophes. The "overcoming" of the one-sided character of the economy is due to the intervention of social forces or social forces prompted by social consciousness, or by governments. No new order of totality is achieved, that is to say, no new synthesis is brought about. A kind of coexistence is brought about between the momentum of the market economy and regulation based on the idea of service. There is, at the most, a perpetual endeavor to overcome the one-sidedness of the market economy; there is no ultimate, rounded achievement in that direction. This may be viewed as a dialectical move in the "soft" sense of the term. The difference between it and dialectic proper lies in the difference of structure: in one case a totality is achieved, in the other, the maximum achieved is an unstable mutual mitigation of different systems. The market economy is mitigated by the notion of services, the notion of services is mitigated by the benefits attached to and the consequences of participation in the process of production and competition. Although what emerges here is not a synthesis, but only a kind of cutting of edges of each system, it can be placed within the range of the meanings of "dialectic" because the awareness of the pitfalls of the one system is the promoting factor in the emergence of the other, the alienating, system.

3

Hegel's system with its formal structure of dialectic is the most prominent case of dialectic proper, even though the concept itself is inherited, obviously, from Greek philosophy. In the broad sense, dialectic in Hegel's version is – as in Plato's – "a guide on the voyage of discourse, if one is to succeed in pointing out which kinds are consonant and which are incompatible with one another."[6] Hegel is aware of his affinity with Plato, an affinity which at least extends to Plato's presentation of a positive dialectic as distinct from the negative one which is common to Plato and the Sophists. This negative dialectic mixes up that which is in the representation (*das Vorgestellte*) with

[6] *Sophist*, 253b.

concepts, while the positive dialectic resolves contradiction without blurring them. The difficult and true thing is to show that that which is the other (ἕτερον) is the same, and that which is the same (ταῦτον ὅν) is an other, and this from one and the same angle (*Rücksicht*).[7] We turn now to the exploration of Hegel's theory of dialectic by way of an analysis of the formal structure of his dialectical discourse.[8]

4

The problems involved in the nature, structure and laws of dialectic were not sufficiently elucidated by Hegel himself. It is true that he laid down the main objective of the dialectic and on the basis of his findings we can reach some conclusions about it. But certain formal problems remain unsolved. For example, what is the logical relationship between the various shapes of the process, or how do the various terms involved stand in relationship to one another? Nicolai Hartmann remarks that Hegel left the dialectic in the region of "*Ansich*" and that he did not raise it to the region of "*Fürsichsein.*" That is to say, the dialectic lacks self-reflection; it has not analyzed itself or determined its own underlying laws and structure. In a word, Hegel's dialectical system lacks – paradoxical as this may sound – a fully developed theory of dialectic. Allusions to such can be found, but these do not form a systematic theory, so that an attempt to analyse Hegel's dialectic must be based upon the dialectic itself, not on hints regarding its nature which happen to be found in his writings. But such an attempt does not mean to impose a uniformity which does not exist. The method employed by Hegel was not a rigid one and cannot, therefore, be reduced to a few formal points. For this reason it is possible to explain it only in principle, without entering into secondary questions. We shall deal with the content of the system only insofar as it affects the formal structure, so that it will be possible to make clear the nature of dialectic as such, apart from the specifics of the system. An attempt to analyse the formal structure of Hegel's dialectic does not imply that dialectic as such is simply a method or that it is identical with its formal structure. The dialectical system is based on an interaction between the substantive evolvement of concepts and the delineated logical stages of that evolvement. This qualification must

---

[7] *S. W.*, XVIII, pp. 222–223.

[8] Consult: Eduard von Hartmann. *Über die dialektische Methode.* Zweite Auflage. Historisch-kritische Untersuchungen (Bad Sachsa 1910).

be borne in mind while we try to abstract, as it were, the formal structure from its actual immersion in the system. As we have said, this
abstraction is justified because it will bring out some particularities of
Hegel's system as well as underline formal considerations operating
in that system.

Points to be raised are these: Is there any logical necessity for the
precedence of thesis to antithesis in the process thesis-antithesis-
synthesis? Are thesis and antithesis disjunctive alternatives, and is the
synthesis the logical ground on which this disjunction rests? And if
the synthesis is indeed this logical ground, is it warranted to speak of a
dialectical *process* at all?

We shall consider now the problems implied in the structure of
dialectic from the point of view of each of the three terms or stages in
turn.

## 5

### A. THE THESIS

We begin with the first thesis of the Logic, i.e., Being. Are we to
consider Being as occupying a determinate position in its own right,
that is to say, does it form the absolute beginning of the process so
that the whole process depends upon and is based on it, or is it only
one stage between others, without a unique position? The second
alternative is clearly preferable, since the *Logic* is based on the previous
account of the manifestations of Spirit[9] set out in the *Phenomenology*.
It is only by reason of previous development that Being can be seen
as the first thesis of the *Logic*. But if this is the case, then this first
thesis can form a beginning only with respect to subsequent steps.
In other words, the thesis forms a relative rather than an absolute
and unconditioned beginning.

We may ask further: if pure Being is not the absolute beginning
of the dialectic, are we correct even to consider it as the first thesis
of the Logic? The answer seems to be this: pure Being is placed where
it is, not by virtue of itself but by virtue of its relation to pure *knowledge* as abstract knowledge. Pure Being devoid of any qualities is the
complement of pure knowledge lacking special content. It is immediate
Being, i.e., abstract Being. It is simple unity without any determination
or content, paralleling the simple unity of pure abstract knowledge.

[9] *Logik*, I, p. 53 (I, p. 81).

Pure knowledge also lacks any relation to content and is confined within its own limits. But knowledge confined within its own limits and lacking any content ceases to be knowledge. Pure knowledge is simply immediacy.[10]

Thus it is obvious that Being does not form the absolute beginning of the system, because we reach it through knowledge which does not apply itself to qualities and determinations. If we eliminate the relation between knowledge and content and confine knowledge to itself, it becomes empty and as such cannot have any specific character. In its emptiness knowledge becomes a neutral entity, abstract and immediate; henceforth there is no distinction between knowledge and Being. Knowledge becomes Being, but not as the result of the dialectic which gives fullness and concreteness. It becomes Being because it is empty of other relations, therefore the Being it becomes is pure Being. Thus, pure Being ceases to be independent because it owes its being to knowledge; and knowledge is the basis for the positing of Being. Pure Being, too, becomes a neutral element, devoid of qualities and specificity; it is only that with which the process of qualification and specification starts.

It is clear that we cannot consider the first thesis as the absolute foundation for the system. Beyond it lies pure knowledge which does not enter into the dialectical process once it becomes pure being.

If the first thesis is not the beginning of the system, we can even less consider as an absolute beginning the other theses developed within the dialectical progress. These theses are determined within the progress, that is to say, they are products of syntheses preceding them. Thus we have no reason to consider the theses as having the character of absolute beginnings within the dialectical system.

The result of this negative conclusion is that the thesis which does not form the absolute beginning of the dialectic cannot be its subject. L. George considers the terms developed through and within the dialectic as predicates of a subject serving as the foundation of the system.[11] The subject of the dialectic cannot be the first thesis because the position of subject implies a difference between subject and predicate. Therefore the terms which follow the first thesis, being developed from it within the dialectic, cannot be predicates of this thesis. Moreover, the first thesis itself is a predicate of the Absolute,

---

[10] *Logik*, I, p. 53 (I, p. 82).
[11] L. George, *Princip und Methode der Philosophie mit besonderer Rücksicht auf Hegel und Schleiermacher*, Berlin 1842, p. 67.

thus making all the terms laid down by the dialectic predicates of the Absolute. No special position can be attributed to the first thesis. Rather, dialectical progress can be considered as a development of predicates defining the Absolute, which development constitutes both the result of the dialectic and the beginning of it.

The objection may be raised that in spite of all we are compelled to consider the thesis as the first step even if it is not the absolute beginning. In relation to all the steps which succeed it – it constitutes a beginning, and is therefore prior to the others and precedes them. But what do we mean by this priority? At best it is one of time, therefore only of a subjective character. If we analyse the dialectical process from the subjective point of view, i.e., if we ask how the various terms manifest themselves in our consciousness and how we reach each term in our thinking, we can say that "thought develops only because we are thinking it."[12] Within our consciousness there exists a stream of ideas one of which succeeds the other. The subjective consciousness is ruled by time, so that we can speak in this connection of priority, precedence and succession. Thus only from the subjective point of view can we consider the thesis as the first term in the stream of cognition. But this subjective point of view cannot apply to the objective relations between the terms. The terms and their relations are not laid down against the background of time, and therefore time cannot constitute an immanent component of the structure of dialectic. In this sphere, priority in the temporal sense is excluded. Can we consider the thesis as the primary stage from the logical point of view? It seems that we must deny this too.

The aim of dialectic is to give "immanent connection and necessity to the body of science."[13] The stress is on the idea of connection, or in other words, the idea of the whole or totality. The truth is the whole, and each particular determination receives the justification and verification only from its connection with and coherence in the whole. The particular determination cannot be autonomous; it cannot be defined within its own limits, and its truth cannot be inherent in itself. The particular determination is but a transition to the whole. The dialectic rests on the assumption of the whole, so that if every determination takes its meaning and justification only from its connection with and relation to the whole, it is obvious that within the dialectical

[12] J. E. Erdmann, *Abhandlung über Leib und Seele, Eine Vorschule zu Hegels Philosophie des Geistes*, Neue Ausgabe by Bolland (Leiden 1902) p. 21.
[13] *Encykl.* § 81.

system no particular determination can hold an exceptional position.

But the dialectic rests on the doctrine of truth as a whole, meaning that individual and independent truth is denied to a particular determination. Then the thesis in dialectic cannot be an independent stage and cannot be considered as the beginning of dialectical development. It is absorbed in the totality. The whole is a simultaneous entity. All its determinations are interrelated, and they coexist beyond the stream of time. Thus no peculiar precedence and priority can be attributed to the thesis.

In fact, within the Hegelian notion of dialectic, and especially within the forms it assumed in Marxism, two different views regarding the nature of dialectic seem to be confused. Engels writes: "Dialectic ... comprehends things ... in their essential connection, concatenation, motion, origin, and ending ..."[14] The whole world, natural, historical, intellectual, is represented as a process, i.e., as in constant motion, change, transformation, development; and the attempt is made to point out the internal connection that makes a continuous whole of all this movement and development.[15] In this conception as explained by Engels, no precise distinction has been made between the two motifs of *interrelation* and *process*.

Curiously enough, even G. Lukács does not realize the problematic character of the shortcut from ontology to history, though we can assume that he was not deliberately following in the footsteps of Engels.[16] Lukács plainly says that Hegel plays for Marx a preparatory role (we shall come back to the question of the relationship between Hegel and Marx in the final chapter of this work). We are referring now only to the shift from ontology to history. According to Lukács, Hegel, to be sure in his own way, conceived of ontology as history, since the ontological structure of the world evolves and retains self-annihilation, achievements, etc. This type of ontology, according to Lukács, unlike a religious ontology, is a development from its most simple stage which moves upwards to the most complex objectifications of human culture, whereas the religious ontology starts from the divine and moves downwards to the world and to human beings. Yet Lukács, too, seems not to be aware of the questionable nature of the assumption that this character of explication from the simple to the full is to be

---

[14] F. Engels, *Socialism, Utopian and Scientific* (Chicago 1918) p. 3.
[15] *Ibid.*, p. 85.
[16] Georg Lukács, "Zur Ontologie des Gesellschaftlichen Seins," *Neues Forum*, Feb.–Mar., 1971.

read as history proper. Actually, when we assume the identity between the ontological and the historical, what occurs is a shift from one realm to the other. The most one can say is that history proper is rooted in ontology, but this rootedness does not imply the coincidence between the two realms. Lukács apparently tried to find a way, that paved by Hegel, for Marx's concern with history as a basic fundamental human realm. Marx starts with human beings, and not with an essence or substance whose explication travels, among other paths, *also* through human beings. Marx does not read ontology as history but substitutes history for ontology.

Yet we must reiterate that the difference between explication on the level of concept and process on the level of history was not clear to Hegel himself. This is especially so in his *Philosophy of Spirit*, with regard to the shift from Spirit to history, as we have seen. In the *Philosophy of Spirit*, Hegel considered the relation between the different spheres of art, religion and philosophy – not only from the point of view of their place in the system, but also, and perhaps mainly, from the point of view of the dynamic relation obtaining between them, i.e., of the transition from one to the other.[17] For this reason Hegel attributed to each sphere a superiority over the one preceding it. The synthesis constitutes a sequence of links, and not a system of elements posited simultaneously. But it is not necessary to confuse the two motifs of dialectic and to identify totality with process as Engels did. Moreover, the shifting of dialectic from the domain of knowledge to the domain of history requires the addition of the factor of time.

Succession is an essential ingredient of the dialectic of history. But there is no necessity to transfer dialectic into the domain of history if we deal with it as a method forming a system of concepts and ideas. This system is not set up against the background of time and the terms forming the system are not historical factors which can develop in time only. We cannot, therefore, accept the necessary connection between the dialectic of concepts and knowledge, on the one hand, and that of process and succession on the other. The former is timeless and bears a simultaneous character. In a system based upon simultaneity, no priority can be attributed to the terms, and within it, succession in any temporal sense is meaningless. We cannot attribute a logical priority to any one term – the thesis, for instance – because the nature

[17] *Encykl.* § 553–574.

of dialectic is interrelation, and this involves the abolition of the independence and isolation of the specific terms. It is thus obvious that the thesis does not occupy a rounded position within the dialectic of knowledge. Here, with regard to the first aspect of the formal structure of dialectic, we encounter the whole set of problems inherent in Hegel's system.

At this point it is apposite to take issue with a suggestion made by Michael Kosok in his attempt to present a formalization of Hegel's dialectical logic. As Kosok views it, Hegel's logic occurs as a temporal process or procedure. Or, to put it the other way around: "... non-dialectic logic is a-temporal, corresponding to a view of the universe as essentially determined and *given* in 'space,' and merely in need of *description.*" According to this interpretation the various elements to be generated by the dialectic cannot all be present at any particular stage. It follows that we are not dealing with an already formed and determined universe of discourse. We are dealing with a universe of discourse that is in the process of being formed. Therefore, the system is intrinsically incomplete.

This interpretation is indeed adequate insofar as it underlines the fact that the universe is not formed but is being formed. Precisely the shift or elevation from substance to subject, the principal concern of our analysis, is the case in point. The two concepts – substance and subject – exemplify the to-be-formed character of the universe. Once this has been emphasized, it has meaning to say that before the full formation of the universe the universe is incomplete. One may then say that the incomplete cannot be described, because any description will present at the most a snapshot of the static moment and will be unable to refer to that which is to be achieved in and through the process of formation and completion. Yet the usage of the term "space" in this context seems to be rather metaphorical, since space as simultaneity or coexistence does not preclude the inner movement within space.

The metaphor of space was, however, introduced in order to point to the antithetic correlate of space, that is to say, time: either space or time, and if not space then time. But this disjunction seems to be unwarranted. The movement in Hegel's dialectic from one category to another, from being to becoming or from substance to subject, is not a movement in time. Instead of "description," explication has to be applied. The antithesis is inherent in it, but the relation of inherence is not a relation of a change occurring in time. The self-explication of the inherent is not a succession occurring in time. Succession in time may be a kind of model or parable for the relations pertaining to the stages of the dialectical system. But there is a basic difference between a model and an intrinsic content. One has to agree that Hegel himself was to some extent the cause of this wavering between time as a model and time as an infrastructure of the system.[18]

## B. THE ANTITHESIS

Two central problems are connected with the delineation of the position of the antithesis within the dialectic:
(a) the character of the transition from the thesis to the antithesis, and (b) the nature of the opposition of the two to one another.

If, as we have just concluded, the thesis does not occupy the position of a beginning, it is impossible to suppose that the antithesis is deduced from it. Both are on the same level, the thesis being no more general than the antithesis, and the antithesis not being a more particular term. Admitting the simultaneous character of dialectic, the relation between thesis and antithesis is not a relation according to the scheme of a scale. It can be described only as a mutual assumption, i.e., in their opposition, the thesis implies the assumption of the antithesis while the antithesis implies the assumption of the thesis. From the point of view of content, each term eliminates the other.

A remark must be made here regarding content. The content of the antithesis is determined by the content of the thesis. For example, if pure Being is placed as thesis, the antithesis is not a particular quality or predicate because the antithesis must belong to the level of the thesis; in this case, the antithesis is "Nothing." Thus, a kind of priority belongs to the thesis from the point of view of content. This priority is connected with the nature of the thesis as a positive assumption which precedes the negation of the antithesis – in the case at hand, we get Nothing as antithesis. But this side of the relation between the terms concerns only the content of the antithesis (and in particular, the relation between the "first" thesis and the "first" antithesis, because only the first antithesis implies an absolute negation), and has no bearing at all on its formal character. Priority in respect of content does not imply any dependence in respect of form, i.e., the level of

---

[18] See: Michael Kosok, "The Formalization of Hegel's Dialectical Logic" in: *International Philosophical Quarterly* VI, 1966, pp. 596ff. The analysis of the temporal character of the dialectical system is to be found on pp. 606–607.

the terms. From the point of view of form both thesis and antithesis are equal and are involved in mutual relation. As a matter of fact, Hegel accepts the conception laid down by Fichte concerning the relation between the first two principles of the *Wissenschaftslehre*. In respect of content, the non-Ego depends upon the Ego because it is defined as the negation of the Ego; nevertheless, the non-Ego does not depend upon the Ego in respect of its form, i.e., the very assumption of this term is as necessary as the assumption of the Ego.[19]

Similarly, in spite of its dependence regarding content, the antithesis is independent in form because the assumption of the antithesis as a term is independent. Hence it is possible to sum up by saying that the mutual dependence of the two terms relates to content and not to form.

It is impossible to lay down an *a priori* criterion that will decide which of the two – thesis or antithesis – is the thesis or antithesis. If both are necessary and one does not depend formally upon the other, we can change the sequence and consider the antithesis as thesis and *vice versa*. The dependency in content is also reversible. We can, for instance, consider "Appearance" as thesis and from there reach "Essence" as correlate, and thus posit Essence as antithesis. But if Hegel's system is based on the assumption of the positive and essential elements – Being, Essence – as thesis, the decisive factor is the motives underlying the content of his system and not the logic of the formal structure of dialectic.

The problem of the nature of the opposition between the terms has always been one of the central problems in the criticism of Hegelian dialectic. Thus Trendelenburg[20] objected that the opposition of thesis and antithesis does not fit into any scheme used in formal logic. According to such a scheme, the opposition would be a formal and logical one, i.e., a contradiction. If we lay down two propositions – S is P, and S is non-P – there is no possibility that the synthesis of the two would make any sense; that is to say, the synthesis of two contradictory propositions cannot serve the dialectical progress. On the other hand, this opposition cannot be a contrariety, because such an opposition is an opposition in the realm of reality. This would mean that we move the dialectic from the realm of pure thought to the realm of content. But in doing so we misinterpret the nature of the

[19] J. J. Fichte, *Grundlage der gesammten Wissenschaftslehre*, in: *Fichtes Werke*, ed. F. Medicus (Leipzig, n. d.), Vol. I, p. 297.
[20] *Logische Untersuchungen* (Leipzig 1870), Vol. I, pp. 44, 56.

starting point in the Hegelian dialectic. Dealing with this problem, Betty Heimann[21] arrived at some conclusions of great importance. These must be accepted in the main, with some further comments.

Betty Heimann considers the opposition between thesis and antithesis in the Hegelian dialectic as being in between contradiction and contrariety. It is similar to contradiction because one term is the negation of the other, and it is similar to contrariety because the two terms are positive. The opposition between thesis and antithesis is an opposition of two positive terms which negate each other. This will be clearer if we connect it with what we have said about form and content in relation to thesis and antithesis. From the point of view of form the two terms are independent of one another, while from the point of view of content one depends upon the other. In the realm of content the positive character of the antithesis corresponds to its formal independence, and in the realm of form the contradiction corresponds to dependence with regard to content. Because the antithesis is independent and an indispensable term in the dialectical system, it is as positive as the thesis. On the other hand, we must consider the content of the antithesis as determined by its relation to the thesis just as the content of "non-black" is defined merely in relation to "black." In this sense the antithesis has meaning only in relation to the thesis.

An additional observation must be made about this double aspect of the relation between thesis and antithesis, i.e., the double relationship of form and content, and contradiction and contrariety. The two terms form a complete disjunction, for instance, "Being" and "Nothing," "Something" and "Another." Each pair of terms exhausts all the logical possibilities in its respective sphere. This can also be said of the terms in the sphere of essence: "Essence" and "Appearance," "Substance" and "Accidents," "Law" and "Appearance" subordinated to it, etc. From this additional point of view we may say that the relation between thesis and antithesis is similar to that between the two terms in contradiction, since they likewise exhaust the range of logical possibility. On the other hand, both thesis and antithesis are positive, and thus comparable to the terms in contrariety.

Summing up we may say: the opposition between the thesis and the antithesis is not confined to one direction. The two are independent, yet interdependent with respect to content. Both are positive, and one negates the other in spite of its positiveness. They form a disjunction.

---

[21] *System und Methode in Hegels Philosophie*, (Leipzig 1927) p. 329.

We must conclude, therefore, that the dialectic does not lie merely in the necessity to assume two opposed terms, but also in the character of the relation implied in this opposition – the independence and the dependence. The dialectical system consists in the connection of terms and propositions. The terms connected are positive and the connection itself implies both the independence and the dependence. We do not exhaust the nature of dialectic thought if we consider merely the opposition. We must explain the dialectic that lies in opposition as understood by Hegel, because opposition as such is not a dialectical relation. There is no possibility of comparing the relation between the terms in dialectic with the relation between terms in a deductive series. The latter is characterized by single direction and dependence on the first supposition. The structure of dialectic is fundamentally different; while formed by the mutual relation of the terms, it lacks a first supposition. The relation between the terms is one of mutuality, and this mutuality is the source of dialectic because it implies both independence and dependence.

This does not mean, to be sure, that Hegel established the relation between the thesis and the antithesis by using the logical relations of contradiction and contrariety. We have used these relations merely for heuristic reasons, having found the relations in contradiction and contrariety an instructive guiding principle in the analysis of the relations in dialectic.

What can we say with regard to the first antithesis – the "Nothing?" We have said that all the antitheses are of a positive character, but a qualification must be added: with the exception of the first. The first antithesis is a negative one with regard to its content, that is to say – using the distinctions elucidated above – it is independent from the point of view of form, dependent from the point of view of content ('Nothing" is the negation of "Being"); but its content is a negative one. From this point of view we are right in saying that the first antithesis occupies a special position. This is explained by the very nature of dialectic; all the determinations of dialectic are posited within the system, so that the negation of the assumption of terms can also be assumed only within the dialectic. But the first negation, by virtue of its character, is of a peculiar nature, different from all other terms. *"Nothing" is a principle opposed to the very assumption of contents, i.e., a principle opposed to the dialectical system in its substantive sense.* For this reason we must attribute to it a unique position within the system. Here the system touches its own frontier because

within the system and by it the very negation is assumed. This negation is not made in the final stage of dialectic, but at the beginning of it.
Here at the beginning, where there exists only the decision to consider
it, the pure negation, as an opposition to the assumption of contents, is
determined.[22]


## C. THE SYNTHESIS

The dialectical relation, i.e., the relation of dependence and independence between thesis and antithesis, characterizes the synthesis. The
synthesis is the superior or the primary term, the ingredients of which
are the two interrelated disjunctive terms. In other words, the synthesis, compared with the thesis and antithesis – with the exception
of one antithesis – is the more general term, but in spite of its generality
it is the term full of content. In Hegel's terminology, the synthesis
is the more concrete term. From this point of view the synthesis
can be considered to be the higher state with respect to the other
two.

The central problem concerning the place of the synthesis in dialectic is whether it precedes the thesis and antithesis or whether it can
be assumed only on the basis of the two disjunctive terms. If the latter
is true, then the content of the synthesis is defined by the content
of the preceding terms, whereas the development of the thesis and the
antithesis is *a priori* because their opposition is *a priori*. Yet this
procedure cannot be applied to the dialectic of pure thought. It would imply the posteriority of the synthesis. But we have seen that the dialectic
is characterized by the priority of relations, which makes it necessary
to consider the synthesis, which is a relation, as prior to the thesis and
antithesis.[23] The disjunction, i.e., the very relation between the terms
exhausting the range of logical possibilities, means that the range
itself precedes the particular terms. Induction cannot give the totality
of logical possibilities; totality precedes each particular possibility.
Therefore, thesis and antithesis are merely particular manifestations

---

[22] J. E. Erdmann, *Grundriss der Logik und Metaphysik*, Halle 1864, § 80, *Inhaltslosigkeit*.
[23] Professor S. H. Bergman called my attention to the conception of *Gegensetzung* (mutual
assumption of opposed terms) as developed by Salomon Maimon in: *Versuch über die
Transcendentalphilosophie*, ed. princeps, (Berlin 1790), pp. 113–115 and pp. 255–257.
Maimon says that reality and negation are correlative terms and that only through a proposition may we assume each of the two terms. The conception of priority of synthesis and
of the mutual assumption of opposed terms is implied in this view.

of the content of the synthesis. But the nature of these manifestations is marked by their special character as disjunctions.[24]

Thus, dialectic must be considered as a development of terms from *a totality of logical possibilities preceding the particular terms, so that each pair of terms in its sphere constitutes a complete disjunction of the logical possibilities.* The relation between synthesis on the one hand and thesis and antithesis on the other, can be compared with the relation between synthesis and analysis as defined by Kant: the synthesis is the primary term and the disintegration or analysis presupposes the synthesis, because where understanding did not combine it cannot dissolve.[25] This main feature of Kant's conception of synthesis as preceding analysis finds its way into the dialectic of Hegel. The idea of interrelation constitutes the nature of dialectic, so that the synthesis, i.e., the relation, bears the character of priority with respect to the thesis and antithesis as relata.

In any case, it is clear that the scheme of time does not conform to the structure of dialectic. In this connection we cannot consider dialectic from the point of view of succession. We could speak of succession only if the synthesis succeeded the thesis and the antithesis. The scheme of time cannot be adapted to the peculiar relation between the three terms whereby the development of the synthesis seems like a *reversion* to a stage preceding thesis and antithesis. Thus, an analysis of the formal structure of dialectic confirms the doubts expressed before concerning the shift from system to history and from history to the system – this is the topic of the Excursus.

This point of view sheds an additional light on the general character of the system. The system bears a character of retrogression, that is to say, all the terms and determinations are directed toward the starting point. The Absolute begins with itself and arrives at itself. Dialectic is a method of assumption of syntheses preceding theses and antitheses, with every particular assumption expounding the concealed content of the Absolute. The Absolute, the final result of the system, does not

---

[24] It seems that this view regarding the relation between disjunction on the one hand and contradiction and contrariety on the other, can be confirmed by what was said by Hegel in connection with the disjunctive judgement: "The so-called contrary and contradictory notions should really not find their place until this point, for in the Disjunctive Judgement the essential distinction of the notions is posited ... as concrete universality is itself also the *principle* of negative unity ..." (*Logik*, II. pp. 298–299, II, p. 291). This conception regarding the sphere of judgement can also be applied to the relation between the terms in dialectic – as analysed above. This disjunction is the presupposition of the opposition, or, in other words, it is the logical condition of the differentiation of thesis and antithesis.

[25] *Kr. d. r. V.*, B 130 (Kemp Smith, p. 152).

succeed the system's particular terms; it precedes them. One must ask, therefore, what a final *result* means in a system based on retrogression, and what importance can be attributed to the method of development of particular terms if the synthesis of these terms precedes their development. The understanding of dialectic, as well as of the sublation of substance to subject, depends on the elucidation of this problem.

## D. IMMEDIACY – MEDIATION

The place of dialectic within this system based on reversion or retrogression is connected with the pair of terms Immediacy – Mediation. Dialectic starts with a given synthesis. It develops the content of this synthesis through the assumption of disjunctive terms, the thesis and antithesis. In this way it determines, instead of the given or *immediate* synthesis, a mediated synthesis developed through an analysis. Taking into account the history of the problem we can connect the conception of dialectic as a method of reaching mediated syntheses with the problem of genetic definition. The aim of genetic definition – as elucidated, for instance, by Spinoza in *Tractatus de intellectus emendatione* – is to explain the way in which the qualities of an object develop. Genetic definition does not take the thing as a datum, but determines the manner of its genesis.[26] Dialectic, like the genetic definition which comprises not given qualities but the law of their genesis, does not accept given syntheses but develops them through the relation between thesis and antithesis. The development through disjunction of syntheses which precede disjunction – that is the meaning of mediation in dialectic.[27] It can be described as substitution of given syntheses by developed ones. From a historical point of view it is worth observing that this conception may be described as a combination of Platonic and Aristotelian motifs. The knowledge is knowledge of contents that are *given* (Plato) and at the same time a development of the implicit content (*an sich*) to its *telos* (Aristotle).

There exists a difference between genetic definition and dialectic which throws light on the character of the Hegelian system. Genetic

---

[26] E. Cassirer, *Das Erkenntnisproblem in der Philosophie und Wissenschaft der neueren Zeit* (Berlin 1911), vd. II², p. 89.

[27] The above distinction between two kinds of synthesis explains why the Logic of Being is considered as an immediate sphere as opposed to the Logic of Essence as a mediated sphere. The syntheses in the sphere of Being are immediate in respect to the syntheses in the sphere of Essence, as the latter are in respect to the syntheses in the sphere of Concept. The shift from substance to subject is a shift from immediacy to mediation.

definition – as can be seen with Spinoza – is directed toward a construction of terms and geometrical forms. Genesis means the *determination of the way of construction*. The dialectical method is not a constructive one. It does not, in place of the given synthesis, assume another one in a new sphere. The aim of the dialectical method is to *develop* the given by discovering its implicit or concealed content. It is an *explication*, not a *construction*. Together with the principle of development from immediacy to mediation, another law functions here – that law making the mediated immediate.[28] The developed synthesis is put in the place of the synthesis which preceded the development. Mediation also means development from a state of untruth to a state of truth,[29] since truth amounts to fullness. Thus, the non-constructive nature of dialectic leads us back to problems we encountered regarding the content of the system and the nature of philosophy, where the formal problems cannot be isolated from the problems of content.

6

The distinction between "softer" versions of dialectic and the "hard" version is now clearer, because we have taken Hegel's version of dialectic as a paradigm for our understanding of what dialectic is. If it is a process of intro-regression, a shift from the immediate beginning to the ultimate end, which in turn is the beginning insofar as it evolved its inherent and latent content – then in this sense Plato's dialectic will not meet the criteria of Hegel's dialectic. Plato is concerned with the exploration of essential shifts occurring between kinds, or, with the affinity between Forms. Plato's point of departure is the overcoming of the isolation of concepts or Forms. This is present in Hegel, but Hegel goes beyond it. Real, actualized affinity comes to the fore when we start with relations and not with relata, or when we start with a synthesis and move from a less articulate immediate synthesis to a more and more articulate mediated synthesis, winding up with ultimate synthesis. At least one of the criteria for the achievement of the end lies in the awareness of the identity of end and beginning, though they differ as the mediated differs from the immediate or the articulate from the inarticulate. We could say that dialectical evolve-

---

[28] N. Hartmann, *Die Philosophie des deutschen Idealismus*, Zweiter Teil: *Hegel* (Berlin 1929), p. 266.
[29] J. E. Erdmann, *Grundriss*, etc. § 10.

ment in Hegel is Plato's recollection written large – not the process of recollecting performed by the soul, but the process of bringing to the open the contents already there in the beginning but not yet made explicit. The system is based on the rhythm of coming back.

Our own "coming back" brings us to substance and subject, in terms of Reason and Spirit, necessity and freedom, etc. It is clear that Hegel's system is characterized by a very stringent notion of coherence. The formal structure of the dialectical shifts is a restatement of the substantive shifts occurring with the particular categories and concepts of the system, while the substantive shifts might be looked upon as exemplifications of the formal structure of dialectic. There is no distinction between system and method. The method, says Hegel, is the consciousness about the form of the inner self-movement of the method's content.[30] It is the content in itself which moves the content forward, and which is the dialectic of the content.[31]

This concatenation of system and method, rooted in the character of Hegel's enterprise, carries with itself the difficulty of being too systematic. One might venture to suggest that in Hegel the openness and the closedness coincide. To some extent, the system removes the momentum of wondering. Marx's theory – could we really speak in the Marxian context of a theory? – raises some renowned objections to this character of Hegel's system. We will now examine Marx's relation to the philosophy of Hegel – after an excursus about concept and time.

[30] *Logik*, I, p. 35 (64).
[31] *Ibid.*, p. 36 (64). Karl Rosenkranz puts this notion of the nature of method as follows: "Hegel's method of speculation would not be what it is, that is to say the self-development of the state of affairs, were it to be treated as an external form for everything, as a *passe-partout*. Only in identity with the content does it have truth." (*Psychologie oder die Wissenschaft vom subjectiven Geist*, Königsberg 1837, p. XII). Consult: Dieter Henrich, *Hegel im Kontext*, Frankfurt a/M 1971.

# CONCEPT AND TIME

### I

The emergence of subject out of substance, or rather the emergence of substance as subject is, as we have seen, the running thread of Hegel's philosophy and of his dialectical endeavor. Hegel is not motivated by strict epistemological considerations alone, that is to say, by the desire to overcome the gap between substance as given and subject as knowing the given. He is motivated by the entire program of philosophy as he sees it: the ultimate end and interest of philosophy is to reconcile thought, concept, with actuality.[1]

The stumbling block in this endeavor of reconciliation is time. Once the notion of actuality is introduced, time cannot be brushed aside. In the course of our previous analyses we have come across *vis-à-vis* history proper and *vis-à-vis* philosophy in the systematic sense some of the problems inherent in Hegel's attempt to establish continuity between the levels of concept and time respectively. We will now deal with this issue more systematically, though critically just the same. The topics of history and history of philosophy will be incorporated in our attempt.

### 2

Let us first be more specific about the time-component in the program of reconciliation between concept and actuality. The question can be put as follows: Where is the isomorphic structure or the homology which permits *prima facie* the assumption that concept and time are capable of identity, and not only of rapprochement?

There are several terminological devices which Hegel uses with re-

[1] *S. W.*, XIX, pp. 684–685.

gard to the potential identity between concept and actuality, a potential identity which ultimately leads to full and actual identity. Terms or metaphors like "development of the Spirit," or "self-elevation of the Spirit to its truth"[2] do point to a vague notion of time, implied or to be explicated.

It is because Hegel's description of the nature of the concept is suggestive of the time-component, that he believes he can move to point to explicit relations between concept and time. To be more specific: development or self-elevation in Hegel is clearly related to self-annihilation, to what he calls "*sich aufheben.*" Now he says about time, that time is the existence of this continuous "*sich aufheben.*"[3] Furthermore, the development or elevation of the Spirit comes about by way of negation of the given and the negation of that negation. Parallel to this, Hegel says about time that it is the negation of the negation and the negation related to itself.[4]

Yet we cannot point to this isomorphic structure between concept and time while disregarding Hegel's own emphasis on aspects of time which are peculiar to time alone, and have no parallel in the structure of the concept. Alluding to mythology, Hegel speaks about the destructive Chronos.[5] It is out of the question to say that the structure of concept carries the destructive tendency within it. The destructive tendency, if there is such, is neutralized by the conserving character of concept; every more developed categorial stage entails in itself the preceding categorial stage.

Hegel is aware that because of this "Chronos" aspect of time, time is the form of restlessness (*Unruhe*), and he lists in the traditional way the most prominent aspects of time: being one after the other (*das Nacheinandersein*), becoming and disappearing, summing up this latter aspect of time by saying: "The temporal is while it is not, and is not while it is."[6]

Yet, the philosophical program of identity between thought and actuality leads Hegel to affirm not only that some aspects of Spirit do become known in the process of time from the point of view of the knower, that is, the human knower, but also that these manifestations in time are indeed manifestations of Spirit from its own side. There is no way to reconcile the two views: the temporal character of actuality

[2] S. W., X, p. 17.
[3] S. W., IX, p. 78.
[4] Ibid.
[5] S. W., IX, p. 80.
[6] S. W., X, p. 322.

from the viewpoint of the human knower and the intrinsic need of Spirit to manifest itself in time and to become fully developed actuality through this manifestation, that is, to become substance elevated to subject.

Historically speaking, Hegel struggles here with some of the problems that preoccupied the Neo-Platonists in their theory of time. For Hegel, however, actuality is structured as a series and not as a vertical-emanative hierarchy, which leads to the assumption that fundamentally there is nothing external to the self-propensity of thought or Spirit. Things, he says, are what they are – through the activity of the concept which inheres in them and which reveals itself in them.[7]

Looking at a more immediate background to Hegel's position, let us recall Kant's theory of Schematism. For Kant, time is a mediator between the categorial apparatus of concepts on the one hand, and the data of sensibility on the other. In Kant's view the *tertium quid* between concepts and time is order. There is an order of time in the very sequence, and at that, parallel concepts or categorial concepts do fulfil their function in ordering data in modes of functional relations. It is not by chance that, unlike Kant, Hegel did not place the emphasis on order. He placed the emphasis on self-negation. His ultimate philosophical objective in terms of the speculative rationality of the world was fulfilment and not ordering, identity and not relations, self-enclosed synthesis and not open-ended progressive cognition moving from hypothesis to hypothesis. Hegel's notion of rationality molded his view of time, both in his choice of which features of time he would bring into prominence, and in his incorporation of manifestation in time into the inner character of Spirit, rather than into the limited scope of human cognition. There is thus a tacit polemic against Kant in Hegel's own theory together with an explicit attempt to overcome the limitations Kant imposed both on categorial concepts and forms of sensibility.[8]

3

In addition to this positive, or else negative, continuity of philosophical tradition which we encounter in Hegel *vis-à-vis* the relation between

---

[7] S. W., VIII, p. 361.

[8] Consult on this point the present author's: *Experience and its Systematization, Studies in Kant*, The Hague, 1965, p. 164 (Second edition 1972).

the level of concept and the level of time, there is most probably a rather complex religious theme revealed or concealed here: the religious interpretation of Hegel is important in his own eyes, as it is well known, and it became one of the decisive factors in the development of post-Hegelian philosophy.

We suggest that one has to distinguish between Hegel's motivation and Hegel's system. Even when we take Hegel's own expression literally, that is, that he is after "the speculative Good Friday" (*der spekulative Karfreitag*)[9] we cannot disregard the fundamental ontological difference between Good Friday as an event in time and a – or the – speculative rendering of Good Friday. Perhaps Hegel means to say that the presence of God in the world as an event personified in Christ, parallels the character of the speculative as the necessity to be in its own concept.[10] Moreover, Hegel tries to identify the mysterious component in religion with its speculative component.[11] But this is precisely the question: whether this identification or elevation gives proper account of the character of the mysterious element in religion. There is an interpretation of religion and there is a self-interpretation of religion, and these two are by no means identical. To deal seriously, that is to say philosophically, with a religious world view is to see it not only in terms of its potentiality for the fully developed philosophical approach, but also in terms of the religious world outlook as such in its own immanent phenomenology. It is not enough to say that mysteries are secrets for understanding (*Verstand*) but not for reason (*Vernunft*). Only a philosophical position which presupposes that all human creations converge in an ultimate human creation, which is philosophy, can assume that the mystery of religion is to be elevated and thus fully conceived on the philosophical level, thus making the historical Good Friday into a speculative Good Friday. But something more is asserted here: in the religious mystery man faces the transcendent; in the speculative interpretation of the mystery transcendence is not faced, but enclosed in the self-development of the Spirit. In the religious mystery man receives a message, while in the speculative dimension he interprets what he has received, elevating it to the full articulation of a philosophical world view. The real dilemma we face here is whether philosophy is reflection on subject matters or the fulfillment of reflection emerging out of substance. Because Hegel took

---

9 *S. W.*, I, p. 433.
10 *S. W.*, II, p. 53.
11 *S. W.*, XVII, pp. 111–112.

the view that reflection inheres in substance, he saw time as a manifestation of Spirit and religion as a prolegomenon to philosophy.

The fact that Hegel imposes on the conept of reason or Idea notions like *Ehre* and *Herrlichkeit*, sheds some light on the motivation of his thought and points to the influence of the current climate of opinion. But the logic of the system itself, the transformation of the *"Karfreitag"* onto the speculative level prohibits the super-imposition of relegious notions on the systematic and dialectical evolvement of concepts.[12]

4

We may go a step further and suggest a distinction in general terms between Hegel's concept of God and the religious interpretation or background of that concept. Hegel understands self-consciousness as being for itself (*Fürsichsein*) fully accomplished. The aspect of relation to the other is removed from self-consciousness once it reaches its ultimate position, since there is no external object to be related to. Thus, self-consciousness is the nearest example of the presence of the infinite. Yet Hegel identifies self-consciousness at its peak with God, since God is for himself as he is and, by the same token, that which is for him.[13] Hegel is here expressing the traditional view of the self-contained nature of God; but let us not forget that religion proper is a relation to God from the human end. The descent of God to man takes place against the background of the difference between God and man. Thus either Hegel sees self-consciousness as only the nearest example of the infinite and this makes it impossible to identify self-consciousness with God as self-contained being, or, he retains the self-contained nature of God which makes God's affinity to man not only a mystery but unnecessary. Even when Hegel is motivated by religious associations, he makes religion categorially obsolete, since the ultimate for Hegel is not the relation of man to God, but the relation of God to himself. This is not merely to echo the traditional controversy in the Hegelian school about the position of religion in the system, but to point out Hegel's wavering between self-consciousness as resembling God and self-consciousness as identical with God.

We face here the intrinsic limits of the dialectic system once that

---

[12] Consult: Robert Minder: "'Herrlichkeit' chez Hegel ou le Monde des Pères Souabes" in: *Etudes Germaniques*, Juillet-Décembre 1951.

[13] *Logik*, I, pp. 148–150 (I, 171, 173).

system is understood not as a pursuit of the affinity of concepts but as an established totality imbued with self-cognition. There are some rather important components of this system which have been left not fully articulated, in a semi-developed state, in order to achieve their expression of the system. The issue of human and divine self-consciousness is the most prominent case in point.

Hegel speaks in the same breath about man reaching the consciousness of the infinity of his Spirit and about subjectivity arriving at the consciousness of its infinity.[14] But there is no basic categorial necessity to assume that man's consummation amounts to the full evolvement of subjectivity up to the level of infinity. Man's reflective subjectivity can be maintained *vis-à-vis* the realm of objects without assuming that subjectivity steps up to the level of divine existence and nature. This leap from subjectivity in its maximum consummation to subjectivity as immersed in infinity is obviously related to Hegel's attempt to view the existence of man in time and history as a manifestation of God, as *manifestation* and not as *creation* only.

The same ambiguity comes to the fore when Hegel says that the divine has to become in me and through me. The deed of the cult is the existence (*Dasein*) of God in me; the cult is the movement of God to men and of men to God.[15] Now, it goes without saying that it is very difficult to maintain the view that cult is a movement of God to man. Cult is a human enterprise, aimed at giving expression to man's *religio*, to man's approach to God. Hegel must make cult a two-way movement because of his view that the divine is immersed in man and *is* through man, so that the whole process of bringing God to man and man to God is both a human process and a divine process at the same time.

The concept of God as traditionally rendered cannot suffice for a comprehensive dialectical system. Hegel had to ask himself whether he gives a speculative meaning only to *Karfreitag*, or rather whether he gives a speculative meaning to God, thus going beyond the concept of God. This would lead him beyond the religious frame of reference, since the concept of God would itself be viewed only as a step toward an ultimate synthesis, and God himself not as a being identical with that synthesis. The fact that Hegel clings to the concept of God has its explanation in his background, as well as in his system: the concept of God is conceived and rendered in historical religions.

[14] S. W., XV, pp. 252–253.
[15] S. W., XV, p. 256.

Henceforth the movement or evolvement from historical representations to speculative interpretations has its foothold in the pendulum swinging from religion to philosophy and from philosophy to religion.

Even more important, it is not only that religions are historical entities, and that the movement from history to speculation or from time to thought can be exemplified in historical religions. Since in Christianity God entered history, God as such, and not only religions, has historical connotation; the shift from history to speculation embraces not only religions but the very concept of God itself. Yet willy-nilly Hegel imposes on himself a conceptual limit. Only because he assumed that God is the ultimate synthesis could he stop at the concept of God and view that concept as philosophy's ultimate rendering of notions adumbrated in the progressive manifestations of Spirit. As a matter of principle he could have gone beyond this assumed ultimate synthesis and rendered God hyperspeculatively, or he could have done to God what he did to *Karfreitag*. This, of course, would have led him even further from time and history than he actually went.[16]

A passage from Karl Rosenkranz, who in this respect follows in the footsteps of Hegel and by the same token exposes the system to the criticism concerning us here, provides an appropriate resume of the preceding analysis of the alleged continuity from concept to time. Rosenkranz says: "History is the recollection of the shapes which the Spirit has already given itself. *It* (i.e., history) *becomes a science through the cognition of the necessity of those shapes.*"[17]

Two separate, though interconnected, issues arise in this context: can history, elevated to the level of science, make us realize the necessity of its shapes, make us recognize, for instance, that Greek philos-

---

[16] On problems related to Hegel's Philosophy of Religion consult: Kenneth L. Schmitz, "Hegel's Philosophy of Religion, Typology and Strategy" – *The Review of Metaphysics*, 1970 X 717ff.

See also: Michael Theunissen, *Hegel's Lehre vom absoluten Geist als theologisch-politischer Traktat*, Berlin 1970. Theunissen tries to show that Hegel translated the trend of Christianity into Platonic and Aristotelian metaphysical concepts.

On the question of the relation between concepts and time, compare Kenley R. Dove, "Hegel's Phenomenological Method," *The Review of Metaphysics*, 1970, mainly p. 619.

My own feeling is that the interpretation which leads to a view that there is not that much of a gap between the level of concept and the level of time is very much under the influence of the contemporary Existenz-Philosophy and the importance or even preponderance of time within the world view of that type of philosophy. There are signs, as at least one reader read them, that Hegel becomes a philosopher whose system is getting incorporated into different systems whose "primary intuition" differs from that of Hegel.

[17] Karl Rosenkranz, *System der Wissenschaft, Ein philosophisches Encheiridion*, Königsberg 1850, p. 513.

ophy was a necessity, Christianity was a necessity, Luther was a necessity within Christianity, the French revolution and the English parliamentary reform were necessities? The second issue is this: suppose that Absolute Spirit entails in itself Greek philosophy, Christianity, the idea of freedom, etc., how come that these ingredients become historical shapes proper, that they do occur in time and at a certain point within a certain sequence in time? Why should the emergence of subjectivity be a subsequent event after the emergence of the concept of substance, to quote only one example from the history of philosophy? Couldn't it be the other way around? Ultimate synthesis could be achieved from the position of subject leading to the position of substance, though Hegel presents the achievement of ultimate synthesis as a movement from substance to subject, both conceptually and historically. After all, the self-consciousness of Absolute Spirit is from the very beginning in possession of that synthesis, and in that initial synthesis there is no priority to be assigned to either pole. To be sure, from the point of view of the final subjects and their efforts it really matters whether the progress moves from one or another pole. The achievement of the finite subject carries within itself the effort leading to the achievement. Even when we grant that ultimate synthesis is necessary and is within reach, the procedure which brings it about may be, to say the least, more flexible. Hegel, and Rosenkranz echoing him, do not grant this possibility. Once they present the conceptual exhibition and the process in time as in full conformity, they assume total necessity: the ingredients are necessary, the synthesis comprising them is necessary, and the method is necessary, too. Method is understood here, as it were, literally: it is not only a procedure, it is a way, and a way taken in time. And that is the question.

# CHAPTER SEVEN

# ABSTRACTION AND CONCRETENESS

## I

With regard to the notion that the main concern of philosophy is totality – and we take that notion as expressing Hegel's view – we may distinguish three major positions. The first is represented by Spinoza. In this position totality qua substance is the point of departure of the metaphysical system. Substance-totality is that which is in itself and is conceived through itself, that is to say, it does not depend on data outside itself. As a matter of fact, there are no data outside the totality. Substance as the beginning of the system is known by the philosopher who reaches the level of intuitive knowledge.[1]

The second position is represented by Kant. Totality is the unconditional, and as such cannot appear in experience since experience is an encounter of data in time and space and thus an encounter of data conditioned by the forms of perception. Experience is knowledge of relations and nothing can be removed from the network of relations. Totality is at the end of the regression or progression from conditions to conditions. But we cannot assume that that end is within our reach. The unconditional as the Absolute is not a non-thing (*non ens*) but it is only a thing-of-thought (*Gedankending – ens rationis*). These entities are sometimes called *entia ficta imaginaria*. The formal contradictions or antinomies which accompany attempts to state the unconditioned in a definite cognitive assertion instead of in an open series of conditions, are but the formal index of the impossibility of knowing totalities.

The third position is represented by Hegel. As against the dichotomy of knowledge and the open series which never closes – because as soon as we arrive at one condition we move to a further one and are bound

---

[1] *Ethics*, Book V, Proposition XXIV and the following propositions (Elwes, Vol. II, pp. 264ff).

to do so – Hegel has a continuous shift from statement to statement and to totality embracing all the statements formulated *en route*. This is the meaning of the infinity which is composed of parts; the infinite character of totality does not lie in its open-ended character, but in its ultimate coming back to its own point of departure. Realization of totality is realization in Spirit, since there can be no realization of totality lacking thinking. Thinking and its character as problematic move the process of realization up to ultimate resolution. Since time does not have an independent position in Hegel (we have elaborated this point before), extension in time cannot be considered an obstacle on the route of Reason coming back to itself, to its initial home. For Kant totality expresses an unfulfillable aspiration; for Hegel, it expresses fulfilment. The realization of totality on the level of thinking assumes the character of thinking. Thinking in Hegel has an all-pervasive and assimilating character: whatever is thought as an object becomes a content of thought.

There is another aspect of Hegel's system which relates to realization of totality. Dialectical description starts with the first thesis of Being or with the concept of Essence *versus* its manifestations. The ultimate realization of totality, in turn, is to take place on the level of Being or on the level of Essence, while Being becomes enriched by evolvement and Essence is enhanced by the absorption of its own manifestations. Awareness of the contractions and limitations which pertain to each penultimate stage in Hegel's system is the factor which produces the movement toward realization. Thus, thinking has to be absorbed in Being and Essence. It cannot remain in a subject whose position is that of a merely external observer overlooking the game of dialectic. Thinking must eventually inhere in the position attained by the dialectic: thinking is mediation, the stage we arrive at is mediated by thinking, so that the stage we arrive at has the character of thinking. This is another statement of the shift from substance to subject.

This mode of realization is for Hegel "speculation," since for speculation finitudes are radiants of the infinite focus which emits them and is at the same time built of them.[2] In categorial terms, the meaning of this metaphor expressing the principle of speculation, is the identity of subject and object.[3]

The reconciliation accomplished in and by speculation is the true arrival at the concrete. The abstract is finite, the concrete is the truth, i.e.,

---

[2] *S. W.*, Vol. I, p. 68.
[3] *Ibid.*, p. 35.

the infinite object. Philosophy is the outspoken enemy of the abstract
and leads back to the concrete.[4] This is so because the concrete is the
unity of opposite determinations; it is the universal which entails its
own other.[5] While in concreteness determinations are brought together,
in abstract thinking they are separated and placed in isolation. To take,
for instance, something as internal only is to take it abstractly; thus the
internal is only external.[6]

Abstractness pertains only to thinking entangled in finite determinations. Full actuality as totality is concrete, and by definition cannot
be abstract. Totality is the unity of subject and object; as such it is
achieved in the final manifestation which leads to the conclusion that
totality and concreteness are virtually synonymous.

Here lies the root and the groundwork of Marx' position *vis-à-vis*
Hegel's and *vis-à-vis* philosophy in general. Marx carries over the
concept of totality and its actualization. He questions, to put it mildly,
the level of actualization allegedly achieved in thinking, Spirit, subject,
Absolute, etc. Our next point will deal with Marx' attack on the
abstract character of philosophy as he understood it.

2

Actuality in Hegel amounts to concreteness and is thus opposed to
abstraction. Hegel understood abstraction – mainly – as the isolation
of different determinations belonging to a whole. Concreteness is the
bringing together of the determinations, following the motto of the
true as the whole. The concrete is not the sensuous, tangible thing in
space and time which as such stands in opposition to the abstract
"concept." Abstraction is legitimate on the way to knowledge of the
concrete insofar as it bears on the distinction between the essential
and that which is appearance only. Abstraction intends to point out
the essential by separating it from its involvement in mere external
appearances. Yet abstraction justified thus far, cannot be justified as
ultimate procedure since the ultimate stage of knowledge and actuality
is the bringing together of both essence and appearance. This bringing
together of the separated aspects is the shift to concreteness. Again we
see how, for Hegel, to be entertained in thought is concreteness; both
abstractness and concreteness imply intentionality. On the level of

---

[4] *Ibid.*, Vol. XII, p. 10, Vol. XVII, p. 53.
[5] *Ibid.*, Vol. XVII, p. 109.
[6] *Ibid.*, Vol. XV, p. 392.

abstractness thinking is incomplete, while on the level of concreteness it is complete, that is to say, identity of subject and object and knowledge of that identity is established. To move to the level of thinking is, for Hegel, to move to the level of concreteness.

Marx attacks this position. He does not accept the view that speculation is identical with concreteness. The fundamental and persistent stamp of abstraction is to be entrapped in thinking. No methodical sublation of stages in the dialectical procedure can possibly remove this basic trait. Hence actualization on the level of thinking is a contradiction in terms; the totality of Hegel's subject is an abstract one. Actual existence for Hegel is, as Marx says, the abstraction.[7] There is, in Hegel's view, no human self. There is only the abstracted and fixed self,[8] fixed being a separated, self-contained entity.

The main concern of Marx's attack on Hegel, and also on Kant, as we shall see, is not the reality of the external world but the reality of the human being, who cannot be immersed in a totality constituted by reflection. The real subject remains as before outside the mind in his self-sustained position. This is so as long as the mind takes the speculative stand, the theoretical only. The subject – which may also be a society – continuously vacillates a mere presupposition before a representation (*Vorstellung*).[9]

Marx comes back at this point to Kant's analysis of abstraction. We should not say, Kant remarks, "to abstract something" (*abstrahere aliquid*), but "to abstract *from* something" (*abstrahere ab aliquo*). Hence what goes by the name of abstract concept is in point of fact an abstracting concept (*conceptus abstrahendus*).[10] For Hegel, abstraction is the isolation of particular determinations which belong together; for Marx, following out the trend of Kant's thought, abstraction is the detachment of concepts from the locus of all determinations and from the given totality of determinations, that is to say, from the actual existence of the subject.

The shift toward reflection is bound to be an abstraction for Marx, and no dialectical exploration can possibly talk away that original sin of speculation. Furthermore, along with abstraction and speculation goes the depersonalization of the concepts and categories employed.

---

[7] "Ökonomisch-philosophische Manuskripte" (1844), in Karl Marx – Friedrich Engels, *Werke, Ergänzungsband* (Berlin 1968) Erster Teil, p. 572.

[8] *Ibid.*, p. 572.

[9] "Einleitung zur Kritik der politischen Ökonomie," in Karl Marx – Friedrich Engels, *Werke*, (Berlin 1961), Vol. XIII, p. 633.

[10] Kant I.: *Logik*[3] (Leipzig 1920), p. 103.

The human being is himself turned into a category. History is an abstraction which we talk about. But actually, history does nothing. It is no possessor of tremendous wealth and it does not fight battles. It is man, the actual living man, who does all this, who possesses and fights. It is not history which takes advantage of man, using him as a means; history is but the activity of men pursuing their own goals.[11]

The separation of man's qualities from man himself is the root of alienation. Every alienation involves the positing of a new hypostasis – indeed in Kant's sense of hypostasis: taking that which exists only in thought to exist as an actual object outside the thinking subject. It is the fallacy of making one's thoughts into a state of affairs (*Sachen*).[12] In Marx's own language, this fallacious procedure which underlies hypostatic thinking and thus alienation, is not only characteristic of Hegel. It is characteristic of all philosophy because philosophers have turned predicates into subjects.[13]

This criticism of abstraction, and along with it of speculation and philosophy in general – as essentially relying on the procedure of abstraction – implies the rejection of Hegel's notion of sublation (*Aufheben*). Marx rejects the well-known idea of Hegel that sublation has the double meaning of negation and conservation. There can be only negation, Marx argues, and no conservation. Actual existence cannot be preserved on the level of reflection. Hence the locus of the solution of the problems of existence is the locus of the problems, that is to say, existence itself. With regard to this and cognate issues, Marx takes Hegel as paradigm of the philosopher who does not relate to actuality, but lifts actuality up to the level of reflection, eventually creating an imaginary totality. Hence, he says, the *praxis* of philosophy is theoretical and never becomes real *praxis*. Philosophy is a kind of critique which measures a particular existence with the yardstick of essence, or a particular reality with the yardstick of the idea. This brings about the immediacy of a realization of philosophy on the level of philosophy itself, but not on the level of actual existence. This immediate realization is essentially tied up with contradictions, since there cannot be realization outside the locus of reality. Realization has to be taken seriously and should not be moved up to the shadowy world of cate-

---

11 "Die Heilige Familie," in Marx – Engels, *Werke* (Berlin 1958), Vol. II, p. 98.

12 *Kr. d. r. V.*, A, 384, 392, 395 (Kemp Smith, pp. 355, 359, 361).

13 This is the main theme of "Kritik des Hegelschen Staatsrechts," Karl Marx – Friedrich Engels, *Werke* Bd. I, Berlin, 1958, pp. 203ff.

gories.[14] The system of philosophy is turned into an abstract totality. The relation of philosophy to the world is one of reflection about the world.[15] No real identity with the world is achieved in spite of the program of the system of philosophy. From the start, no real identity can be achieved in the locus of philosophy as reflection.

When Hegel's philosophy is exposed to a critique from the angle of abstraction – the critique which Hegel voiced against Kant, for instance – the only alternative is to take philosophy as an external reflection of the world. The more daring is philosophy in its pretension to be identical with the world, the more severe is the critique raised against it or evoked by it. These words, which have absorbed the vocabulary of Hegel, are Marx's. Yet the program is close to Kant's critique of metaphysics. It is immaterial whether Marx was aware of this affinity with Kant. We shall see presently where Marx explicitly relates to Kant.[16]

Marx's conception, or let us say, mistake, is the reverse of Hegel's conception or mistake. Hegel saw the independent position of reflection and turned it into the seal of actuality: Marx denied the position of reflection and forbade any independence to be attributed to it. Only reality is self-sufficient. To be sure, Marx could not explain the activity of consciousness, even to the extent that that activity is related to the needs and interests of the subject, or is ideological in its direction. He blurs the distinction between the activity of consciousness and reflection considered as substantive, and the very activity itself. Do consciousness and reflection emerge from reality? Or do we presuppose consciousness and reflection in order to assume their responsiveness to reality, their serving the needs of reality or of the actual human subjects engaged in reality?[17] Marx turned to the notion of interest to explain the activity of reflection without distinguishing between reflection and its direction in terms of the objects intentionally entertained or in terms of historical processes envisaged.

The primary meaning of the word "interest" (*Interesse*) is "to be involved," "woven in," "to take part in." Kant speaks about "inter-

---

[14] This is a paraphrase of: "Doktordissertation," in Karl Marx – Friedrich Engels, *Werke*, *Ergänzungsband*, Erster Teil (Berlin 1968), p. 327.

[15] *Ibid.*, p. 329.

[16] Marx criticizes philosophy as pretending to be the actuality, while Kant criticizes metaphysics as pretending to know totalities. There is an ambiguity involved in terms of the limitation of reason. Jindrich Zeleny in "Kant und Marx als Kritiker der Vernunft", *Kant-Studien* Jhr 56 (1966), p. 338 misses that ambiguity.

[17] See the present author's *The Human Subject, Studies in the Phenomenology of Ethics and Politics*, (Springfield, III, 1966), pp. 30ff.

est" (*Interesse*) in different senses. One of the interests of which he speaks is that of Reason in its speculative application. This interest is the knowledge of an object up to its highest principles *a priori*. Interest in the practical sphere lies in the determination of the will with respect to its ultimate and complete end.[18] Yet in the area of judgments of taste, that is, aesthetic judgment, Kant narrows down the concept of interest: an object can be very interesting but we do not have an interest in its existence. We do not derive any pragmatic benefit from its existence. Pragmatic interest presupposes or engenders need; the best examples of interest and need in this sense are inclinations toward the pleasant.[19] To come back to the interest of speculative reason: it is connected with the pursuit of knowledge up to *a priori* principles. Hence there is a speculative interest in the knowledge of totalities since in that knowledge we are about to reach the ultimate fulfilment of Reason, and that fulfilment essentially entails the elements and laws of its own application abolishing the dichotomy between laws and data. Reason does not create concepts about objects but orders them with regard to the totality of the series of their conditions.[20]

Yet Kant points out the illusion inherent in Reason, in that sense which takes the subjective representation of a thing as objective, which takes Reason's propensity toward totality for the achievement of totality. The hypostatic fallacy is precisely this projection of the subjective onto reality. It is rooted in Reason's momentum towards unity – in Reason – unto the unity of the universe. Reason has a speculative interest, but this interest cannot be satisfied except by way of "natural and inescapable illusion."

Marx narrows down the concept of "interest" to desire for results, effects of action, expected advantage, well-being, profit and benefit. Interest is self-interest. To be sure, Marx introduces a qualification into this concept of interest when he speaks about "well understood interest," where the private interest of a man coincides with the interest of humanity.[21] We may wonder about Marx's use of the notion of *well* understood interest, since the well-understood presupposes understanding as discrimination, awareness of differences, weighing of notions and avenues of expression and action. Is this activity of understanding an outcome of the interest? The *well* understood

[18] *Kritik d. pr. Vernunft*, ed. Karl Vorländer (Leipzig 1929), p. 138 (Lewis Beck, p. 124).
[19] *Kritik der Urteilskraft*, ed. Karl Vorländer (Leipzig 1924), p. 47, § 5.
[20] B pp. 490ff (Kemp Smith, p. 422).
[21] Die Heilige Familie, *ed. cit.*, p. 138.

presupposes the capacity of preferring one interest over the other; it presupposes the distinction between spurious interest and true interest. Yet Marx does not concern himself with these questions which are implied in his concept of interest. Since he clings to the view that Hegel reversed the order of reality by making reflection not only totalistic but independent, he only puts forward against Hegel a different totality, the area of existence motivated by interests and well understood ones at that.

Once the concept of interest is presented as the search for benefits there is no room left for speculative interest in Kant's sense. The very appearance of an interest of speculative Reason either expresses an interest in possible effects, or else conceals the interest in that sense. Both expression and concealment are motivated by one's interest. Hence instead of the natural illusion of Reason, which is both natural and unavoidable in spite of its being an illusion, there emerges the concept of *opiate*. Clinging to the opiate is a display of a self-interest, that of keeping people inactive or of removing motivation for changing the historical reality, since fulfilment is found in an imaginary reality, as suggested by religion, for example.

We have seen before that Hegel takes philosophy to be the time or age conceived in thought. Hegel could assume this continuity from time to philosophy because time itself is impregnated with ideas. Thus philosophy is the articulation of ideas which are historical realities in the first place. Marx substitutes interest for idea, and maintains that philosophy or theory in general is but an articulation of the socio-economic position of an age, and of its ruling class in particular. There is a continuity from an age to philosophy, though this continuity in Hegel's sense is not justified, since the reality of the age does not have the character of idea but of interest. This is the meaning of the statement in the *Manifesto of the Communist Party*: your ideas are products of the bourgeois production and property conditions and your right is but the will of your class elevated to the position of law, while the content of that will is given in the material conditions of the life of your class.

Marx takes the view that philosophy is the depiction of reality, but he supplements this view by a more extreme position, namely, that once reality is depicted, philosophy as an independent activity loses its medium of existence. At the most, philosophy, as abstracting from existence, can be a summing-up of the most general results, abstractions which arise from the observation of the historical development of men.[22] Marx mentions Hegel's view of philosophy as emerging from the event, the renowned Owl of Minerva metaphor where the philosopher arrives on the scene *post festum*. But he gives this notion his own twist: since the absolute Spirit as the creative world Spirit reaches consciousness only *post festum* in the philosopher, his fabrication of his history exists in consciousness only, in the opinion of the philosopher, in the speculative imagination alone. The act of transformation of society is reduced to the mental activity of the critical critique.[23] Hence if we cling strictly to the view that philosophy and theory are summations of events, nothing real can occur on the level of philosophy. Whatever is real remains in the reality which was articulated by philosophy and from which it abstracted. Philosophy, beyond its inherence in the Spirit of the time or in the sum total of class interests in historical time, is a mere fancy of the imagination.

The evaluation of philosophy as abstraction implies that there can be nothing in philosophy which is lacking to reality. If reality is characterized by a rift between classes and their interests, or if there is a fundamental humiliation of man in reality, then the idea of totality – being a harmonistic whole – is but an invention of the imagination. Marx attacks the idea of totality from independent though mutually assisting angles:

(a) There is a gap between totality and the divided society existing in historical time. Totality is an imaginary achievement. It would defy the position of philosophy as a *post festum* activity, since it would give philosophy an independent content. This criticism of the idea of totality clearly applies to the idea of sublation. A divided reality cannot be sublated onto the level of Idea as a coherent Idea. The split is bound to remain in spite of the Idea since it remains on the level of reality. No reflective transformation can remove it; a full-fledged synthesis is impossible.

(b) The notion of totality is attacked because it replaces reality by Idea, even if reality were not marked with a split. The main question is, how can men still live at all after a total philosophy?[24]

(c) Totality is imaginary, not a totality at all – these are two points made against the understanding of philosophy as tied up essentially

22 "Die Deutsche Ideologie," in Karl Marx – Friedrich Engels: *Werke*, Vol. III (Berlin 1958), p. 27 (*The German Ideology*, ed. R. Pascal, New York 1947, p. 15).

23 "Die Heilige Familie", *ed. cit.*, p. 91.

24 "Hefte zur epikureischen, stoischen und skeptischen Philosophie," 2. Heft in Karl Marx – Friedrich Engels, *Ergänzungsband*, Erster Teil, pp. 215–217.

with the notion of totality. Abstraction is programmatically placed in contrast to the notion of totality: abstraction is abstraction from, i.e., from reality with its split and from the real human beings who preceded philosophy and live after it. Hegel took totality to be an Idea; Marx takes it to be a product of imagination. Insofar as the Idea of totality conceals the factual division in reality, or insofar as it makes us think that there are more important things than the split in reality, the Idea of totality serves an interest, an interest which is opposed to the transformation of reality. It lets us be satisfied with the activity of the mind. If philosophy is abstraction, then it must abstract from, and then there is no guidance in philosophy. There is a second current in Marx's thought about philosophy to which we shall return: philosophy as interpretation is not enough; it has to be realized.

Marx attacks the self-contained character of philosophy. Hegel stressed the interdependence between method and substance. Marx criticizes him for reducing the whole of metaphysics to method only.[25] Hegel assumed that the method is identical with the content, while Marx takes him to task because he assumes method without content to constitute the philosophical system. Whatever occurred and does occur is, for Hegel, precisely that which evolves in his own thought. There is no reality to refer to, thus the philosophy of history is rather the history of philosophy, of his own philosophy.[26] This is a kind of solipsism where reflection is self-contained.

Marx somehow feels that substituting interest for the Spirit of the time is not enough. He suggests a concept of the Spirit of a people in addition to that of the Spirit of the time, mainly in a pejorative sense – and not systematically – applied to the German people. Hegel's philosophy is the "finest expression" of German historiography, for which it is not a question of real, nor even political, interests, but of pure thoughts.[27] The German judges everything *sub specie aeterni*, in terms of the essence of man; others view everything practically, in terms of actually existing men and circumstances. The thoughts and actions of others are temporal, the thoughts and actions of the German are timeless.[28] There is a German propensity to declare that the fact is based upon

[25] "Das Elend der Philosophie" in Karl Marx – Friedrich Engels, *Werke*, Vol. IV, (Berlin (1959), p. 125.

[26] *Ibid.*, p. 129.

[27] "Die deutsche Ideologie", *ed. cit.*, p. 39 (Pascal, 3. 31).

[28] *Ibid.*, pp. 445–446 (Pascal, p. 38).

abstraction. This is how you have to proceed if you want to appear German, profound and speculative.[29]

These and similar statements are part and parcel both of Marx's polemic temperament and of the "climate of opinion" of his generation. His criticism of the German *"Volksgeist"* runs counter to Hegel's claim that with the Germanic stage the Spirit of the world reached its summit. Yet his refuge in the character of a people offers the hint that the concept of interest does not fully explain the Idea of a speculative totality, which presupposes the actuality of the Idea. There is bound to be a characterological or historically accumulated propensity towards blurring the distinction between facts and abstractions. The interest in concealing the interest is supplemented by a national habit of presenting abstractions as self-contained entities.

## 3

The notion that philosophy interprets the world might possibly be accommodated to the notion of philosophy as abstraction. Yet the demand that philosophy be actualized goes beyond the notion of philosophy as abstraction only, even when we remove the pejorative sense which Marx gives to the latter. The demand for realization of philosophy implies that philosophy is not ultimate, that thinking has to come back to actuality. This is the meaning of Marx's saying about the truth of this-worldliness (*Diesseits*). Marx states in a letter to his father, where he sums up his estrangement from the philosophy of Kant and Fichte, that the point he has reached is to seek the Idea in the actual itself.[30] The actualization of philosophy would require that the guiding principles of philosophy would become the guiding principles of human reality and thus cease to be philosophical only – philosophical in the sense of reflective. Hence the realization of philosophy amounts to its sublation, in the strict sense of that loaded term – the negation of the

[29] "Die deutsche Ideologie," *ed. cit.*, p. 469 (Pascal, p. 115). The contention that philosophy as entertained by the Germans is a compensation for the lack of political action in Germany is not confined to the polemic presentation by Marx, or for that matter by Engels. It appears in different forms in Heine as well, and among the middle-of-the-road Hegelians. Consult Hermann Lübbe, *Politische Philosophie in Deutschland, Studien zu ihrer Geschichte*, (Basel/ Stuttgart 1963 pp. 45–46). Here again we encounter a shift from the descriptive to the evaluative understanding of the different *Volksgeister:* The *Volksgeist* of the French has a propensity toward political action, while the *Volksgeist* of the Germans has rather a propensity toward speculation. The polemic starts when a different evaluation comes about: When political action is looked at as being more important than speculation, there is nothing to be proud of in immersion in speculation.

[30] In *Ergänzungsband*, Erster Teil, p. 8.

abstract character of philosophy on the one hand, and on the other, the immersion of philosophy in the real conduct of human beings in historical time: which is the preservation of the content of philosophy while leaving behind the locus of philosophy. The bringing together of philosophy and the world – this is the programme. This bringing together makes the world philosophical and philosophy worldly; it amounts to the realization of philosophy and at the same time to the loss of philosophy.[31]

But once we speak about the realization of philosophy in the historical existence of men, the notion that philosophy is the actualization of the potentiality of Reason on the level of Spirit – the Hegelian notion of the locus of philosophy – undergoes a severe attack, even when this attack is less audible than the attack on abstraction with which we have dealt. Marx could accept the nominal definition of actuality in Hegel's sense as the unity of its possibility and its existence.[32] But he could question the assumption that this unity is to be achieved only on the level of Idea. This unity, to be sure, is to be achieved on the level of time, of the existence in time of human beings, which is essentially social existence. In Hegelian terms we may say: the unity of the possibility and existence is achieved, in Hegel, on the level of Absolute Spirit only. All the stages which precede the level of Absolute Spirit are preparatory stages only. Marx has the actualization of that unity on the level of actuality in time – for Hegel, the level of Objective Spirit – and he rejects the deferring of the actualization to the level of Absolute Spirit. He rejects this deferring for two reasons: (1) an actualization on the level of Absolute Spirit is not an actualization at all, since that level lacks the seal of real being, as it is reflection only, which mirrors an actuality outside itself; (2) if there is to be actuality, it has to evolve on the level of human existence proper, in the network of mutual relations between human beings. It has to penetrate into the character of human social and historical institutions. The actualization of philosophy has to be taken seriously and thus cannot occur merely within the confinements of philosophy as such. If so, what is the sum total of notions or ideas which are and can be realized?

Marx rejects not only actualization on the level of reflection, but also actualization in a world beyond, beyond the scope of action and

---

[31] Anmerkungen zur Doktordissertation in *Ergänzungsband*, Erster Teil, p. 329.

[32] Hegel, *S. W.*, Vol. III, p. 179. On philosophy as interpretation and realization of philosophy in Marx see the present author's *Basic Problems of Marx' Philosophy* (Indianapolis 1965), pp. 91ff. Consult: Jean Hyppolite, *Studies on Marx and Hegel*, edited and translated by John O'Neill, New York and London 1969.

will. This, virtually, is his criticism of Kant. Kant was satisfied with
mere "good will," even when that will remains without results. He
finds the actualization, die *Verwirklichung*, (Marx uses here the same
term and applies it to philosophy in general) of that good will, the
harmony between the will and the needs and urges of individuals, in
the realm of "the beyond."[33]

Clearly, Marx is referring to the resolution of the Antinomy of
Practical Reason in the notion of the Postulates of Practical Reason.
The Antinomy lies in the fact that there is no necessary connection,
sufficient for the highest good, between happiness and virtue in the
world. This connection cannot be expected to result even from the
most meticulous observance of the moral law.[34]

The achievement of highest good is impossible according to the moral
law. Hence, the moral law which commands that it be furthered must
be fantastic. The resolution of this Antinomy takes first a negative
shape: it is not impossible that the morality of intention should have
a necessary relation as cause, to happiness as effect, in the sensuous
world. But this relation of the good will to the actual, i.e., sensuous
world, is only indirect, mediated by the intelligible author of nature.
The achievement of the highest good presupposes the immortality of
the soul which will safeguard the existence of the subject so that he
can enjoy the fruit of his good intentions in happiness. The actualization
of the highest good is beyond the good will and beyond the actual
world. It is a Postulate of Practical Reason, which is not demonstrable
but is still an inseparable corollary of the practical law which is *a
priori* and unconditionally valid.[35]

The Antinomy and the Postulates are rooted in Kant's distinction
between knowledge and will. Knowledge is confined to the data of
sensuality while will creates its expressions by moral intention. It
follows that knowledge is subject to limitations. Marx uses acid and
sardonic language to characterize the thrust of Kant's system. The
Kantians are, so to say, the hired priests of not-knowing; their daily
business is to pray to the rosary about their impotence and the
potence of things.[36]

Marx seems to be not far from Hegel's rejection of the distinction –
or rather dichotomy – between being and ought. Marx wants to estab-

---

[33] *Kr. d. pr. V.*, pp. 131ff, (Lewis Beck pp. 117ff.)
[34] "Die Deutsche Ideologie," *ed. cit.*, p. 177.
[35] *Kr. d. pr. V.*, pp. 140ff. (Lewis Beck, 126ff.).
[36] Hefte zur epikureischen, stoischen und skeptischen Philosophie, 2. Heft, *Ergänzungs-band*, Erster Teil, p. 71.

lish the unity between the potency of Reason and the potency of things. But what is the core of that unity? Here he seems to follow Kant rather than Hegel. Marx's notion of the direction and substance of the actualization of philosophy has a Kantian flavor. Let us quote Kant at length on the "realm of ends":

In the realm of ends, everything has either a *price* or a *dignity*. Whatever has a price can be replaced by something else as its equivalent; on the other hand, whatever is above all price, and therefore admits of no equivalent, has a dignity. That which is related to general human inclinations and needs has a market price. That which, without presupposing any need, accords with a certain taste, i.e., with pleasure in the mere purposeless play of our faculties, has an *affective* price. But that which constitutes the condition under which alone something can be an end in itself does not have mere relative worth, i.e., a price, but an intrinsic worth, i.e., dignity.

Now morality is the condition under which alone a rational being can be an end in itself, because only through it is it possible to be a legislative member in the realm of ends. Thus morality and humanity, so far as it is capable to morality, alone have dignity. Skill and diligence in work have a market value; wit, lively imagination, and humor have an affective price; but fidelity in promises and benevolence on principle (not from instinct) have intrinsic worth. Nature and likewise art contain nothing which could replace their lack, for their worth consists not in effects which flow from them, nor in advantage and utility which they procure; it consists only in intentions, i.e., maxims of the will, which are ready to reveal themselves in this manner through actions even though success does not favor them. These actions need no recommendation from any subjective disposition or taste in order that they may be looked upon with immediate favor and satisfaction, nor do they have need of any immediate propensity or feeling directed to them. They exhibit the will which performs them as the object of an immediate respect, since nothing but reason is required in order to impose them on the will. The will is not to be cajoled into them, for this, in the case of duties, would be a contradiction. This esteem lets the worth of such a turn of mind be recognized as dignity and puts it infinitely beyond any price, with which it cannot in the least be brought into competition or comparison without, as it were, violating its holiness.

And what is it that justifies the morally good disposition or virtue in making such lofty claims? It is nothing less than the participation it affords the rational being in giving universal laws. He is thus fitted to be a member in a possible realm of ends to which his own nature already destined him. For, as an end in himself, he is destined to be legislative in the realm of ends, free from all laws of nature and obedient only to those which he himself gives. Accordingly, his maxims can belong to a universal legislation to which he is at the same time also subject. A thing has no worth other than that determined for it by the law. The legislation which determines all worth must therefore have a dignity, i.e., unconditional and incomparable worth. For the esteem which a rational being must have for it, only the word "respect" supplies a suitable expression. Autonomy is thus the basis of the dignity of both human nature and every rational nature.[37]

---

[37] *Grundlegung der Metaphysik der Sitten* (Leipzig 1897), pp. 60–61. ("Foundations of the Metaphysics of Morals," incl. in *Immanuel Kant, Critique of Practical Reason and other Writings in Moral Philosophy*, translated and edited by Lewis White Beck, Chicago 1949, pp. 92–93).

The distinction elaborated above has to be supplemented by a few additional references in Kant. Price (*pretium*) is public judgment of a thing's value (*valor*) and is related to the trading of diligence. Kant deals with price in the course of a discussion of money, starting off his analysis with a definition of money which, as he says, is a thing the usage of which is made possible only by making it external.[38] Related to this is the distinction between persons and things. Kant says that between man as person and all other things as things (*Sachen*) there can be no relation of obligation (*Verbindlichkeit*). Were a man the only man on earth he would not possess any *Sache* as his property.[39] It follows that to place man on the level of a thing is to remove him from his ethico-metaphysical position. Further, Kant uses the distinction between value and price in connection with what is called character, as we say: this man has "character." To attribute "character" to a man is not only to say something, but also to praise, since "character" is a rarity which evokes respect and admiration. As against this, talent has market value since the owner of land or other property can use such a man in different ways. Hence value is related to that which man makes of himself, and this is the description of his character.[40]

It is our contention that Marx's notion of the realization of philosophy is related to this distinction between value and price in their relation to man. And *pari passu* Marx's criticism of society is related to that historical and sociological misplacement which removes man from his position as end and value in himself, and makes of him a thing with a price and exchange value. Here Marx follows Kant rather than Hegel. We shall now look into the details of his affinity with Kant.

4

Marx does not differ from Kant in the substance of his view about man as a moral end. He differs from Kant first, in adding a historical dimension, i.e. in terms of the history of ideas, to the assessment of the moral position of man. Marx sees the view that man is for man the highest entity as an outcome of emancipation from religion. Religion as a matter of principle subordinates man to a heavenly entity.[41]

---

[38] *Metaphysik der Sitten*, § 31.
[39] *Ibid.*, § 11.
[40] *Anthropologie in pragmatischer Hinsicht*, § 87, 111.
[41] "Zur Kritik der Hegelschen Rechtsphilosophy," in Karl Marx – Friedrich Engels, *Werke*, Vol. I, (Berlin 1958) p. 385.

Yet in speaking about this fundamental position of man and one's attitude toward it Marx uses Kant's term "categorical imperative." The use of this notion at this point is obviously justified, since one of the formulations of that imperative is the command always to relate to the humanity in one's own person as well as in any person also as an end, and never as a means only. One of the arguments put forward by Kant for the categorical imperative consists in seeing human existence as having in itself an absolute value; this amounts to its being an end in itself. Moreover, Kant uses the term "value" or "absolute value" and the term "dignity" as synonyms, asserting that humanity itself has dignity (*Würde*). That dignity inheres in the prohibition against turning man, who is an end, into a means. Marx also observes that value and dignity (*Wert und Würde*) are fully related to each other, both by etymology and by meaning.[42]

Further still: the distinction introduced by Kant between value proper and exchange value, or the value of person and the value of thing (*Sache*), underlies Marx's assessment of the position of man in the existing bourgeois society. The labourer, says Marx, becomes a commodity the more he creates commodities. There is a direct proportion between attribution of value to the world of the thing (*Verwertung der Sachenwelt*) and the diminution of the value of the world of man (*Entwertung der Menschenwelt*). Labour does not produce commodities only; it produces itself and the labourer as a commodity. The essence of the labourer turns into a means for his existence or subsistence – if we may introduce here a term that Marx does not employ in this context but which is implied in his use of the term existence.[43] Not only is the language that of Kant, but the ideas behind the language are also Kant's, both with regard to the distinction between ends and means as well as the distinction between different meanings of "value."

Man's involvement in the world of exchange value means his involvement in the realm of money as the external expression of the activity of exchange. Extending his characterization of religion as the subjugation of man to a power beyond him, which power is only a projection of man, Marx speaks ironically about the divine power of money.[44] Very much to the point is his comment about Kant's criticism of the ontological proof of the existence of God and the

---

[42] Randglossen zu A. Wagners "Lehrbuch der politischen Ökonomie," in Karl Marx – Friedrich Engels, *Werke*, Bd. Vol. XIX (Berlin 1962) pp. 372–373.
[43] *Ergänzungsband*, Erster Teil, pp. 511, 516.
[44] *Ibid.*, p. 565.

example Kant uses in that context – that of a hundred talers. In a half ironical and half serious vein, Marx says that the real talers have the same existence as the imagined gods. Does the real taler have an existence but in the representation?[45] As a matter of fact, this is not a comment on the character of existence as an involvement in relations as Kant has it – and this is the gist of Kant's criticism of the onto-logical proof of the existence of God; that proof places existence as a predicate and thus not as an involvement in a nexus of relation. Marx's is a comment about the subjection of man to a projection, i.e. – money, which places him in the world of things.

Yet there is a difference, and a fundamental one at that, between Marx and Kant.[46] The difference lies in their respective evaluations of the realm of empirical existence. Or, to state it negatively, it is related to Marx's rejection of abstraction. Marx says that Kant is indifferent to the way man as an empirical subject takes his stand *vis-à-vis* the categorical imperative.[47] Kant does not put forward, according to Marx, the way in which adherence to the categorical imperative moulds the empirical subject. Since Kant disregards that aspect of the categorical imperative – his adherence to the dichotomy of sensuous reality and pure Reason is bound to lead to a dichotomy of the will and the empirical subject – we may conclude that there is no realization of the categorical imperative in Kant, or, broadly speaking, no realization of philosophy. The only realization Kant may claim is respect for the moral law, but not the shaping of reality. There is in Kant the expectation of fulfilment in the world beyond but not a coherent world here and now, based on fidelity to man's essence in present reality. It is instructive indeed that in the context where Marx speaks about the categorical imperative making man the highest entity for man, he moves immediately to his own version of the categorical imperative: to overturn all the circumstances in which man is a humiliated, enslaved, forlorn and loathed entity.[48] The em-phasis should be placed on a turning over (*umwerfen*) following from the categorical imperative. Kant formulates the categorical imperative as a command to "do your deed." Since empirical reality, as it is, defies the directive of the categorical imperative because it has man as a

---

[45] *Werke*, Vol. I, p. 371.
[46] K. Vorländer, *Kant und Marx, Ein Beitrag zur Philosophie des Sozialismus* (Tübingen 1926), is unfortunately not very helpful in exploring the real relations pertaining here, in spite of the promising title of the book.
[47] Hefte zur epikureischen stoischen und skeptischen Philosophie, *ed. cit.*, p. 87.
[48] *Werke*, Vol. I, p. 385.

commodity and not as a value, the turning over is the first step to be taken toward the realization of the imperative, or toward the realization of philosophy insofar as philosophy teaches the categorical imperative. To be sure, philosophy teaches the imperative in abstract form. Marx takes here Kant literally: if the categorical imperative is a call for a deed, the deed has to be performed in the real i.e. historical situation. This requires the overturn of those conditions which contradict the directive of the imperative. Marx takes from Kant the concept of autonomy, whereby the pure will is both the law and the end of the action of the will. But he translates that concept in a twofold way: (1) where there is no autonomy, but subjugation, autonomy has to be established (2) the immediate expression of autonomy, for the sake of autonomy, is the transformation of the present situation, or the overturning of present circumstances. All subjugation of man presupposes autonomy. It is inherent in the human being, in the human essence, that autonomy cannot be totally overpowered by circumstances.

There is an important difference between Kant and Hegel in their views of man. Marx is closer to Kant than to Hegel on this issue. Kant and Hegel speak about the capacity of Reason in man. Yet Kant stresses more the equality of every rational being, precisely in terms of the demand of being and end in itself. Hegel stresses more the elevation of the finite to the infinite. In this process man conceives – theoretically – nature in his Spirit and – practically – he brings about the harmony between the spiritual idea, the good and nature. The preponderance of the practical as Practical Reason is visible in Marx, who follows Kant with the important addition that Practical Reason is intrinsically endowed with the capacity of realizing its ends in the historical world.

Since Marx takes a different view than Kant of the empirical subject's relationship to the categorical imperative, he cannot admit of Kant's clear-cut distinction between the technical imperative and the categorical imperative. He claims that there indeed is a harmony between the interest of the proletariat and the directive of the categorical imperative. The *tertium comparationis* between the two seems to be universality. The categorical imperative is universal since it is based on and addresses itself to the humanity in every person. The interest of the proletariat is universal since it relates to the humiliation of man as man. It thus ceases to be a particular and partisan interest of a class or group of people in a share of the commodities of the world, and becomes an interest directed toward the changing of the world so that a commodity will be a commodity and will not surpass its legitimate boundaries.

Marx deals extensively with Kant's and Hegel's theories of penal law. From the point of view of abstract right, there is only one theory of punishment which corresponds abstractly to human dignity. This is Kant's theory, especially in its strict version as found in Hegel. Hegel does not look at the perpetrator of a crime as at a mere object, a mere slave before the judicial system. He elevates him to a free entity who determines his own position. This is because as a member of society he is also one of its law makers, and has in this capacity determined his own punishment in advance. Yet a closer look at this theory leads to the realization that German Idealism – in this case as well as in many other instances – is merely providing sanction for the present society's set of existing laws by way of supra sensuous arguments. We should not be led astray, warns Marx, when in place of the individual, with his real motivations, involved as he is in numerous social conditions and impositions, the abstraction of the "free will" is employed. Some human features are considered in this theory, but not the human being himself. The theory looks at penalty as a product of the perpetrator's own will. But it is only a metaphysical expression of the old *"ius talionis."* The penalty is nothing else than society's means of defense against violations of its conditions of life, be these conditions what they may. Yet what kind of society is it which does not know a better instrument for its protection than the executioner?[49] Marx approves of the implication of human dignity in penal law, but he rejects that interpretation of penal law which deals with what he characterizes as abstract human dignity, and which, because of its approach, merely reflects an existing social situation. Here two lines meet: (1) abstraction is rejected because it is abstraction only (2) abstraction conceals the real situation behind it.

## 5

Marx is after the realization of philosophy in a special sense. Philosophy as reflection cannot be realized for two reasons: (1) as reflection, it is an immediate realization and, as Marx says (2) reflection cannot be realized in historical time because the two are of different orders and

[49] "Die Todesstrafe – Herrn Cobdens Pamphlet – Anordnungen der Bank von England," in Karl Marx–Friedrich Engels, *Werke*, Vol. VIII, (Berlin 1960) pp. 507–508.

rhythms. As long as we cling to reflection there cannot be realization. Philosophy is to be realized according to the Kantian questions: What should I do? What can I hope for? More specifically, it can be realized so far as it presents a theory of human nature or rather of human value and dignity. In this realization, philosophy has to change its character. It has to give up the dichotomy of Reason and sensuality, of purity and historical time. The realization required by Kant would occur on the very level disregarded by him. We should cease to be priests praying to the impotence of Reason.

Yet this realization amounts to the re-establishment of totality. Spiritual content together with external appearance constitute the totality, as in Hegel.[50] Man can be more than a citizen in two worlds; one world can and ought to be established. Totality is realized in the one human world to be established, and not in reflection – this would be Marx's notion of the realization of philosophy, and of a certain kind of philosophy at that. Thus, with regard to the concept of realization, Marx takes Hegel's concept of totality and superimposes on it Kant's concept of ethical activity.

Hence Marx's analysis of the economic process is rooted in the concept of man and of the realization of the philosophical view of man. It is not enough to say that the misplacement of man as an exchange value is due to man's propensity (*Hang*, in Kant's language) toward evil. Marx explores the processes in which man as a commodity is involved, thus removing evil from the realm of propensity to the realm of history and its processes. Here man is possibly more autonomous than in Kant's view, since man makes himself into what he is. We do not have to trace the perversion to a propensity arising in a realm which contradicts autonomy. Again, once the dichotomy of empirical and rational disappears, the perversion cannot stem from a level which is not part of the essential character of man. Both good and evil have to be explained in terms of the totality which fuses rational and empirical. Hence there is a logic in the perverted position of man and there is a historical continuity of perversions; the economic process is not only an aggregate of evil deeds. Economic activity and economic systems are parts of a kind of Objective Spirit. Here Hegel's notion assisted Marx in tracing delinquent behaviour in terms of Kant's categorical imperative.

[50] *S. W.*, XIII, p. 10.

6

The dialectical character of Marx's theory as against the dichotomic character of Kant's philosophy comes to the fore (1) in the view that the pursuit of interests will eventually bring about the realization of the categorical imperative and (2) that there is a synthesis *qua* totality between Reason and empirical existence.

Marx uses, or let us say, takes advantage of, the concept of totality not only to formulate a notion of the transformation of society. He employs the notion of totality methodologically to bring into relief the rhythm of the economic system. There is an identity of consumption and production; there is a consuming production and a productive consumption. In addition, the relation between these two ends of the economic process is one of mutual mediation. This is a milder form of relationship than the one based on identity between the two. At the same time, production provides the material which is the external object of consumption; consumption brings about the need which is the internal object of production. This "softer" relationship is expressed in the formula: without production, no consumption; without consumption no production.

A still stronger relationship of mediation is found here: each act, while being performed, creates the other; it is the other. Consumption brings to an end the act of production by giving the ultimate finish to the product and by actually dissolving the product. And at the other end, production produces consumption because it creates the particular mode of consumption for what is produced and stimulates the need to consume it. This relationship is dealt with in economic theory as the relationship between demand and supply, or as the relationship between commodities and needs, or that between needs created by society and natural needs. Hunger is hunger, but hunger which is satisfied by cooked meat eaten with fork and knife is a different hunger from that which swallows raw meat with the help of hands, nails and teeth. Interestingly, in this context Marx, too, quotes Spinoza's *Determinatio est negatio* – the proposition we discussed before when dealing with the structure of dialectic. Marx detaches the proposition from its context in Spinoza's system where it concerns the relationship between the infinite and the finite, and takes it as a paraphrase or a metaphor for his thesis: production as determination relates or brings about its negation as consumption and *vice versa*. Marx wants to convey, negatively, the one-sided character of each of the ends of the economic process; positively, their mutual dependence, indeed, their ultimate identity.

This is but an example of what we have named the methodological employment of the structure of dialectic as opposed to the methodological-substantive employment of that structure; that employment leads to the establishment of a new society. The methodological employment is a kind of abstraction in Marx's sense, that is to say, the translation into a categorial concept of processes which take place in reality.[51]

We will sum up the whole analysis. Marx has been introduced into the framework of this study because of the renewed contemporary interest in his works – an interest which at times appears to be an attempt to atone for the sins of omission committed by academic philosophy during the century which has passed since Marx's writings first appeared. We can trace a kind of typology of the four views of totality we have elucidated: (1) Spinoza begins with totality (2) Kant sees totality as the unachievable end (3) Hegel and Marx see totality as within reach (a) of reflection bringing about the identity of itself and reality, or (b) within reach of practical acts of transformation bringing about the realization of the categorical imperative in historical time. There is something in common to both Hegel's and Marx's view here: to be within the totality is to fit. That which does not fit has to be brushed aside. The notion of totality within reach presupposes a kind of survival of the fittest.

The stronger the trend toward rationality, the stronger is the reaction which rises against it. The rejection of totality as program and overriding reality revolves around the axes of various concepts like existence and freedom. Let us bring our analysis to a close with some further observations about Nietzsche, and this is apposite at this point. Interestingly enough, though Nietzsche's references to Hegel are by and large of a moral hue, he also takes exception to some fundamental metaphysical notions, including substance and subject.

Nietzsche objects to the Hegelian tendency to elevate history to the level of philosophy. Hegel's history is simply re-baptized philosophy.[52] This criticism is not unrelated to Nietzsche's moral interest, since he realizes that to present history as progressive self-revelation makes it

---

[51] Einleitung zur Kritik der Politischen Ökonomie, *ed. cit.*, p. 622.

[52] Friedrich Nietzsche, *Der Wille zur Macht*; the quotations are from *The Will to Power*, a new translation by Walter Kaufmann and R. J. Hollingdale, edited with commentary by Walter Kaufmann, New York 1967. Aphorism 412. Will be referred to by numbers only.

of itself surpass moral ideas.[53] He hints at what we spoke about earlier, the theodicean character of Hegel's philosophy, or of German philosophy as represented in Hegel. He relates this to a pantheism "through which evil, error and suffering are not felt as arguments against divinity."[54]

Yet these critical comments do not attack the fundamental stance of Hegel's philosophy. Dealing with the concept of substance, where he mentions Descartes and not Hegel, Nietzsche virtually overturns the sequence of Hegel's dialectic: "The concept of substance is the concept of the subject: not the reverse! If we relinquish the soul, 'the subject,' the pre-condition for 'substance' in general disappears."[55] Thus Nietzsche considers substance as a kind of projection of the subject and not as an evolvement out of a sum total of contents, which is what is connoted by "substance" in Hegel. But Nietzsche goes further: "'The subject' is a fiction that many similar states in us are the effect of one substratum: but it is we who first created the 'similarity' of these states."[56] Here we see the radical character of Nietzsche's criticism. Not only is the concept of substance a projection of the concept of subject, but the concept of subject is itself a fiction. This amounts to the view that consciousness and thinking do not have an independent character, and thus cannot be consummations of totality.

Nietzsche is, in a way, the last link in the chain. What he propagates is the rejection of harmonious, organized totality. That which seemingly fits the totality is not the fittest at all. The fittest is the independent, the isolated, the being who finds his abundance in his isolation. Looking backward at the encounter between Hegelian tradition and its critics, we may say that two ultimate sources have nourished the various expressions of protest: the speculative notion of totality, both in its Hegelian and Marxian forms, is rejected; or else, the character of technological civilization which, though not based on the notion of totality, is just the same interpreted as being totalistic in its systems and organizations, and is rejected in the name of vitality or personal isolation. Both the explicit Hegelian concept of totality and the implicit totality concept of the technological world defy the independent character of the individual and his world.

But here we have already gone beyond an analysis of categorial positions. We moved in the direction of the history of ideas and of Western intellectual history in a broader sense.

[53] *Ibid.*
[54] *Ibid.*, 416.
[55] *Ibid.*, p. 485.
[56] *Ibid.*

# INDEX